BLESS & RELEASE

A Novel By:

RUTH LES SURGE

Copyright © 2021 Ruth Les Surge
All rights reserved.

ISBN-13: 978-1-951503-29-1 Hardback
ISBN-13: 978-1-951503-33-8 Paperback

This book is lovingly dedicated to my beloved son, my cosmic partner and my faithful family and tribe.

To survivors everywhere, and to my divine angels.

Remember that we are all ready for unity consciousness and that we hold within us the highest frequency for humanity.

Table of Contents

Chapter One: Shift Happens 1

Chapter Two: Chocolat Chaud 22

Chapter Three: Fuck This Shit 41

Chapter Four: New Pain 59

Chapter Five: The Secret Sacred Balinese
Women's Masterclass 66

Chapter Six: Meat Hell 76

Chapter Seven: Nada 83

Chapter Eight: Dilly 93

Chapter Nine: Ad Astra 119

Chapter Ten: It's Meditation not Mediation
You Asshole 131

Chapter Eleven: Waiting Games 145

Chapter Twelve: The Big Payback 163

Chapter Lucky Thirteen: Ascension 171

THE CIRCLE

Snow falling, ice sparkling in the density of night
Resting on the ground, under a blanket of flurry
Waiting… Waiting for the end?
Within my bubble, so cold, so numb
Nothing can touch me, not a sound in the air
The forest is lonely, trees whimpering in the wind
It will not be long
Waiting to be gone

Shards of crystal pierce and burn me to my core
There is only feeling,
As I reach for light once more.
Ice smelts, dripping warmth.

Now, I'm one.

By: **Tamsin V.A. Briggs, Spring Solstice, 2021**

Riding the Lit Train The Butterfly Effect Is A Thing; Spirit Hacking, By: Shaman Durek

We are all passengers on this spaceship called Earth, which makes us one global tribe sharing this planetary experience together. Humans are still seeing each other as isolated individual components that are operating independently from one another, because darkness has blinded human perception through the illusion of separation. We must train ourselves to begin to see one another as a 'we', by perceiving each other through the eyes of unconditional love and acceptance. This means instead of identifying others by their differences, and by all the ways they are not like us, and all the ways we are not like them (ek chem - US 2020 election anyone?) We commit to perceiving others by our similarities, and by all the ways that we are alike.

But it's not just about how we perceive other people- it's about how we treat other people. If human beings were to recognize that every person, they see on the street is an extension of themselves in another body, they would have more love, more respect and more reverence for their fellow human. So even while we are still training ourselves to perceive as a *we*, it is important that we practice loving others as we would love ourselves, and that we practice loving others without reservation, and without withholding, and without stinginess and without any less care or quality than the ways we love ourselves.

You Are the Dreamer

We are all creators. Each one of us is constantly creating this reality construct that we are all housed within our will, and our beliefs and our attention. I cannot underscore enough the importance of understanding that we humans are creating our world with our every thought, our every word, our every choice and our every behavior. The way we think, and the way we interact as a collective is quite literally making our world the way it is right now. So, if you want the world to be different, your job is to dream it differently, and to be, and to share, and to radiate every quality you want to see in the world in service to that different dream.

It is our world to fix, tribe. We cannot expect anyone else to do it for us. That means, it is my responsibility just as it is yours to fix the world. That means having the courage to feel the pain of the imbalances that are causing so much destruction in our world. It's not like Gandhi just worked up one day and decided out of the blue that he was going to help liberate his people from the British colonialists. He had to heal something to be inspired to take the action he took. Every leader has to feel the pain of life, because it is the agony of those imbalances that activates our devotion and in return, activates the dormant leadership qualities lying dormant within us. We all exist in some segment of this societal construct, and each one of us has the power to make a difference in that piece of our collective puzzle. Talk is talk; it blows like the wind. To take action, to stand for something we believe in - now, that's meaningful. That's giant.

It's time we take responsibility for our situation on planet Earth. No one did this to us. We did this to ourselves. The day is coming, when we will let go of all distractions as unified global citizens choosing to evolve ourselves and our planet.

The blackout is a blessing. The blackout is an amazing opportunity for us as a unified global collective, to choose to evolve through love, and to choose to evolve through consciousness, and to choose to evolve through our willingness to continue to adapt, and to continue to learn, and to grow so as to become greater human beings, and to become a greater human species that lives in harmony with its resources.

We can choose to be those people, tribe.

Shall we?

CHAPTER ONE

Shift Happens

Somewhere there is a white curtain gently blowing in an open windowsill. This space is calm and frees the mind. A breeze comes in and stirs and billows the thin white cloth and all is serene in this sacred space, gentle and still. This mellow wind comes in; it comes inside her. An emblem of her sacrifice, loyalty, and vision. Pure.

Tell me why, then. Why did they throw her down a dark flight of stairs? Why tie her and bind her and treat her as their servant, never fairly or justly or correctly? Only pretending to care while enjoying her best bits and so casually disregarding and throwing away the rest? Even when she was able and ready and brought the healing right to them. Here, she said. Take this science that can heal the world. But they only saw her torn flesh glistening ripe with her blood, sweat, and tears, before they raped her mercilessly and stole her magic.

Her journey began with light as all the best ones do, as her internal alarm went off, waking her at 5:00 a.m. After the rape, she was destroyed. Beyond her disability (bone crushing spinal stenosis and radiculopathy in her spine—lumbar and cervical), the girl presented as "regular" or "healthy-looking"—whatever that was—and did her best to push on through the pain daily. Still, a girl's gotta work. She absolutely loved her job and, more importantly, she was a natural. So, she forced herself to swing her legs out of bed and felt grateful for her mindset at the start of her day. At first, Big Global seemed to care about employing her as a disabled person. They provided ergonomic workstations and fitted her with proper chairs and let her park in the front, using her government-issued disabled parking pass on particularly painful days. She had always believed in doing something for herself first, before the crazy of the day took over. So, she made some tea, sat, and meditated for just about 20 minutes.

When that was done, she walked back into her cramped room and threw on some yoga pants, a sports bra, and a hoodie, grabbed her earbuds from the charger, scooped her keys and water bottle up from her desk, and headed out for her morning walk. It was the same walk down the same streets she'd been forcing her shuffling feet to do for the last decade. *Boring but stable,* she thought as she gave herself a mental pat on the back for holding it down as a single mother. *Nice job, doing you.* Once back at the house, she checked on her son (still sleeping) and glanced at the clock. It was just 6:31 a.m. Perfect, she thought—she'd have just enough time to shower and get ready before waking him up and getting him ready for school.

She hopped into the shower and thought about her big meeting today. As a rule, the girl tried not to set expectations, but she couldn't help wondering how her presentation would be received. She thought about what to wear and decided on her blue floral Zara dress and her favorite Mary Janes from Paris, last season. She hated that her showers hadn't belonged to her since the night of the attack. As any single mom will tell you, with all the multitasking and responsibilities and moving parts you have going, a long shower and moment or two in the bathroom was the only time and space you really had to relax and let it all go. But ever since that night a month ago, she had not been alone in the shower without them invading her sanctuary, stealing her precious moments of peace. Before all of this shift, she was a rare and beautiful woman who carried the light in her eyes, love in her smile, and wisdom in her bones. She was a powerful, full life force. She gave her house plants names like Joy and Love and Happy and Grace.

But these days her showers became the only place she felt safe to cry and let it all out. She didn't want her son to hear her ugly cry as it might scare him, which meant this was the only place she had to let herself remember. And it scared the hell out of her. She felt the sharp clench of anxiety rising up in her chest, tightening, as her breathing became rapid and she prayed to God to protect her heart and not let her stroke out, leaving her only son, her baby boy, all alone. She was terrified that they—Big Global—would get away with it and she would die from the trauma, naked in the shower, leaving her son without his mother, his only provider, parent, disciplinarian, and chance at a future.

As the panic rose, she repeated a fast limerick:

"Peter-piper-picked-a-peck-of-pickled-peppers!" she spat out.

A trick she had learned from her friend (now wheelchair-bound after suffering a stroke three years before) was that if you ever thought you were having a stroke, you should do these three things: try to smile, check in a mirror to see that your eyes and face are rising up in a smiling pose, and raise both arms above your head. If you could do all three, it was just a panic attack or your mind playing tricks on you. Every day, this was her new shower reality and she hated them for robbing her of precious shower time. Fuckers. She swung the shower curtain aside and peered hard into the foggy bathroom mirror to check her face. She was fine again—until the next shower. The girl was sharp and knew that fine was a four-letter word that began with "F" and was anything but fine. But at least she was going to do something about it today.

She emerged from the bathroom, feeling shaky but clean, walked into her room, and got dressed.

Shit—she needed help with the top button at the neckline and could use some help. She looked at the clock and confirmed it was time to wake her son for school. She walked four feet out of her room, tapped her fingers lightly against the door, leaned in, and said in her best mid-western drawl, "Attention all passengers . . . it's time to rise and shine.".

She walked into her son's messy room and looked down at her giant 13-year-old sleeping boy, sat on the edge of his bed, and began lightly scratching his back.

"Hey there mister—good morning. It's time to wake up, sleepy head."

"Can you scratch my back?" came the sleepy voice facing the wall.

"I already am, and you need to get moving if you want pancakes today," she said.

"Aww mom . . . five more minutes? Please?"

Her son was a brilliant negotiator. His rhetoric absolutely belonged in a courthouse in the future, but for now, the seventh grade was calling.

"Come on, move it please!" she said over her shoulder as she stood up from the bed and walked out of his room, down the long hallways, and into their small kitchen. She loved being in the kitchen and wished she had more time, but she really needed to get them out the door. She still had to go review all her files, organize them, and start the long drive to Seal Beach for her 10:00 a.m. and she still had to do her makeup.

Breakfast was a blur—another handful of supplements and oils, a green smoothie for her, and organic pancakes from Trader Joe's for him with a side of her leftover smoothie. She packed his lunch, fed the cat, and returned to the bathroom to finish getting ready.

Doing her makeup was a pain since her vision had started getting worse from working on the computer all day and night. She leaned into the magnified mirror suctioned onto her regular mirror as she quickly began painting her face. As she reached for the mascara, she thought twice and put it on anyway.

She focused on creating an illusion to disguise the new wrinkles under her eyes. When she smiled, which was rare these days, it strongly resembled an elephant's ass, or so she thought. She dabbed on some serum and concealer, finished by quickly brushing her teeth again, and called out to the boy to put on his shoes.

She darted into her room and grabbed her purse, her laptop, and her briefcase stuffed full of all her files, and checked to look herself over in the mirror. She looked like she always looked and felt like staying in again, but she knew that today's meeting was going to be crucial to her future. To *their* future. So, she did her best to smile at the lady looking back in the mirror, grabbed her keys and threw them in her purse, and walked out to start the car.

Her white Nissan Altima had seen better days. It was a secondhand gift from her parents when she graduated University. She was grateful for the car every now and then, but more so many years ago when it was still new to her and functional. Actually, she preferred to take public transport in metropolitan cities, except on big grocery shopping days or when the weather was bad.

She rolled down her window and honked the horn lightly twice and called for the boy to hurry up and get in the car so they would be on time. He lumbered out of the house, shutting the front door behind him with a thud, walked to the street where their car was, and climbed into the low front bucket seat. He was too tall for this car, she thought . . . well, she would have to do something about that soon. But for now, they had a big day to face and needed to get going.

She began the long drive to drop him off at the backside of his school. They listened to music, both lost in their thoughts. When they pulled up to the curb on the backside along with all the other cars, he reached for the volume button on the radio and turned it completely off. He didn't like attention, this one.

"Goodbye buddy, I love you," she said.

"I love you to mom," he returned without looking at her, unbuckling his seatbelt, reaching for his backpack, and climbing up and out of the front seat.

"Go be somebody! Have a good day and I'll see you here at pickup!" she called after him, as he pulled the top of his hoodie up and over his head and disappeared down the long foggy embankment that led to the nature preserve and eventually to the fence surrounding his school yard.

Still parked along the curb, she looked down at her phone, and entered the address into her maps. It would take her an hour and a half to get to Seal Beach by 10:00 a.m., and it was 8:28 a.m. She was on her way.

By the time she exited the 405, her lower back pain was at a 7 and rising. The combination of her foot doing over an hour of starting again, stopping again on the brake and accelerator triggering her old L5 wounds along with her stress surrounding the meeting she was about to enter was sending throbbing waves of stress to her lower back. She exited Seal Beach Blvd and turned left toward the beach. A right turn onto PCH then a left onto

Main and she had arrived. Parking sucked. She had passed the office on the left and drove down past Nick's Deli—home of the best breakfast burrito of her adolescence back in the day.

She dreamt of ditching her meeting and binging on a machaca breakfast burrito with extra cheese and spicy salsa and getting one of their amazing turkey bacon clubs to go. But instead, she circled the block, found parking in a disabled stall, pulled out her placard from the glovebox, and started to unload her things.

She had a hard time finding the suite—it was tricky. She entered a cute café and had to put all her things down onto the ground, fishing his card out of her wallet, found her cell, and dialed. A woman's voice answered, "Good morning, Ogre & Ogre Law firm, this is Angel, can I help you?"

"Ummm yes, hello. This is Ogre's 10:00 am. I'm here, but I can't find your suite," the girl stated.

"Sure sweetie, where are you right now?" she asked with a genuine tone.

"I'm in a café on the corner. The French one that smells good," said the girl.

"Perfect! You're very close, just go back onto the street, walk up toward the marquee, and we are right above the surf shop"

"Great! Thanks so much, I will be right there." She said and hung up.

She picked up all her things, followed the directions, and found the suite right where the woman said she would. She opened the door, found the stairs, and walked up to the second floor.

It was an old building that had a casual, beachy vibe. *Oh great,* she thought. *I am way overdressed.*

Sure enough, the nice woman was there waiting for her in a spaghetti strap sundress and flip flops.

"Hello sweetie! You found us! Come on in. Here, let me help you with that. Can I get you something to drink? He's expecting you, come right this way," said Angel, the office manager as she led the girl through a short maze of turns, leading her to a big comfortable corner office with a clear view of Main Street and the beach beyond.

The girl's eyes took in the casual beach blue and white décor. His office was cluttered with memorabilia, from hockey and basketball teams to racing. There were awards, a signed platinum record from Snoop Dog, family photos from yachts in the Maldives, degrees from high-ranking institutions, and a stuffed swordfish along the walls.

"Hey there!" boomed a voice from behind the desk. He looked like a large, sunburned Shrek.

"Welcome, have a seat!" he said.

The girl felt uncomfortable until her eye landed on a sign facing her on the corner of his desk that said: "The fucking badass motherfucker sits right here! Fuck off!"

"Nice sign," said the girl. Her eyes took it all in; he was not what she had expected. Sitting across from her was the Ogre, not in any assemblage of courtroom attire, but rather in Bermuda shorts, a Tommy Bahama short sleeve button-down shirt and flip flops. The girl immediately felt overdressed and wished she had dressed more casually.

It was bad enough that she had to be right there, right now, going through this process. The re-telling of her story with Big Global, her wrongful termination, and the rape were bad enough. This caustic retelling was mentally and emotionally exhausting. Maybe that was the way it was meant to be, she thought. Perhaps this part of the experience taught a lesson or released the internal pressure. But also, she felt really uncomfortable sitting here across from a stranger, dressed for a funeral.

They chit-chatted about the last two big cases he won, a similar but different scenario where the victim won millions, and another six-million-dollar payout by a major automotive brand to a young man who had lost the lower part of his right leg. He then shared that he had researched all of the leadership at Big Global and shared his thoughts in brazen racist terms.

"All those Indian motherfuckers are garbage. Slimy rotten weasels," he said.

Then the Ogre started leading the conversation, leaning over his desk while taking notes by hand.

"So, I understand you were brutally attacked by Big Global—is that right?" he asked in a sympathetic tone.

"Yes. That's right," said the girl softly, tears getting stuck in her throat chakra.

"Listen, I know it's painful, and believe me, I've sat here just like you're sitting there a hundred times. I'm going to ask you some questions and see if I can help you get these bastards. "Okay?"

"Okay," she said in a small voice, feeling unsure of how she could possibly pull the story out of her one more time.

The Ogre was a referral from her forensic psychologist. That made her feel a tiny bit better, going into this knowing she wouldn't be ripped off in a cheap Santa Ana office for a deposit like with the last one. No, she had done her research and knew that the Ogre was a badass in his own right. A former corporate asshole himself turned equal opportunity asshole, he apparently had a soft spot for single moms who had been fucked around by greedy corporate cocksucker rapists and considered contingency his act of goodwill and a means to pay for his summer house, weekly trips to New Orleans, and pilot lessons.

He asked her to start at the beginning.

It was impossible to jump right to that awful night without also telling how it all began, explaining how she came to be there in the first place . . . so she went there.

In 2008, as arguably the greatest American president who ever lived, Barack Obama, was running his campaign, he made a call to all single mothers to return to academia. That night, as she was gathered around the television at her parent's house, she, her parents, and her then 4-year-old son, were rooting for Barack, yelling, "GO BAMA!!! GO BAMA!!!" And wouldn't you know, the girl, a previous high school dropout, went and enrolled herself in the local junior college, still working full-time, and three years later earned a full ride to the number one R1 public university in the world. Three years after that, a now published scholar, she was recruited by SHE-E-Os like Sheryl Sandberg, Women of The Channel (WOTC) leaders, and the like. Grateful, she made her choice, and the girl arranged moving services to relocate her and her son to their new lives waiting for them overseas in France, when suddenly her son became very ill and unable to fly.

They were grounded and this rerouted the trajectory of the next three years—enter Big Global. The girl had opened her first LinkedIn professional account and within three days was recruited by Big Global. The rest was history.

"I began for them in August of 2016. And within three months, I was given a promotion in title only, having passed my 90 days probationary period and government background tests. I was appointed a new boss—the CMO and CPO in London. Over the next two years, I worked my ass off, proving my loyalty and work ethic by rising up the ranks, accepting more and more responsibility, finding strategic start-ups and bringing them in as new strategic partners and the likes. I had government clearance, NASA clearance, and international biometric privileges. By the summer of 2017, I ran the global marketing team—again, in title only. I had received one small raise from $24.00 to $27.50 per hour, but with all the overtime and double time, I was still on target to make almost $100K my second year and thought that was great. They knew I worked like a Golden Retriever. All heart—accepting the task, doing the task, returning with a smile for a pat on the head, happy, content, and ready to do it again."

"I was happy there and thought of my boss like my big brother, until the night of my big promotion dinner when he tried to kiss me. That was when instinctively I knew that everything was about to fall apart."

"What happened the night of this dinner?" He asked as he scratched the back of his head.

"It was November 20th, and he had just flown in from Heathrow that morning and had asked me to book whatever restaurant I wanted to for that night, so we could discuss my big promotion. This was a big deal; I'd been working my ass off, proving my worth and rising up the ranks, taking on more and more tasks that fit my skill set and even some that didn't, just to earn a substantial raise. I chose my favorite Italian spot by the lake and also because it was close to my house. We met, and we did discuss business over most of the dinner. But he never produced a contract—although he congratulated me, with cheers and all that. He said his guy in HR would handle the details with me and I believed him. Until then, I had no reason not to believe him. We laughed and caught up and he called an Uber. When it arrived, we left the restaurant and he walked me to my car. We were standing by the trunk when he leaned in to hug me and instead tried to kiss me full on the mouth. I was so startled and shocked, I pushed him back with both hands upon his chest and asked him what the hell he thought he was doing, and he greeted me with catatonic-like silence and a blank stare. Thoughts were racing through my mind as I turned away, mumbling goodnight, and got in my car and raced to get the hell home.

"My mind was reeling with what the hell—why did he do that? Why in God's name would he kiss me? He's married, for

God's sake, with two two-year-old twin boys! He's my boss, why did he do that? No answers came, just more chaos and fear in my gut telling me that my big promotion was about to go all wrong. My big chance at the golden ring was just sabotaged, nearly killing the hope every hardworking, hustling single mother shares. I had worked my ass off earning this opportunity and now this ass hat was going to take it all away. The fear washed over me and turned the heavy food in my belly sour."

"What happened after that?" the Ogre asked.

"That was November 20th. The next night, November 21st, there was an offsite team meeting at a beachfront restaurant in Huntington Beach. I arrived with a female colleague and he was already sitting alone at the bar drinking. That was a long night. That was the night they raped me."

"Tell me everything you remember starting at the beginning," he said, leaning in.

"Well . . ." she took a deep breath in and began at the beginning again.

"I was ambitious, but underpaid, only making about $27.00 hourly plus mega OT, bringing me to just under $100K plus benefits in my second year with Big Global. My BIG promotion was going to give me a base salary of $120K per year plus benefits and BIG quarterly bonuses, IP bonuses, and strategic partner- ship bonuses. The day after he tried to kiss me, he sent emails out, announcing my promotion, introducing me to high level global teams. Mandatory global VC meetings happened all that day, and more verbal promises were made, but ultimately HR evaded me. In other words, things were moving forward as far as Big Global's expectations of my performance, but nothing had been inked. There was no official contract. Just a lot of hype. Combined with my boss trying to inappropriately kiss me the night before, I felt he had absolutely blown to smithereens any real shot at my big promotion coming through as promised." She stopped suddenly and looked down at her shaking hands folded neatly in her lap.

"That was the night they all gang raped me," she said, and began to cry.

The Ogre started calling them "those greedy fucking assholes" and apologizing to the girl.

He said, "No woman should have to go through what you went through," and did his best to be less Ogre-like in this moment. He appealed to me as a father with two daughters of his own and a wife to protect. He said that slime like this "deserved to suffer and pay for what they had done to me." He believed me.

"Go on. You're doing great, "he said as he handed me a box of tissues.

"Meanwhile, meetings continued to be scheduled and my calendar filled, travel was being booked, and I was terrified. This job would have been a huge positive change to any single parent! I went immediately to HR and told them I had two things to discuss with them. They scheduled my meeting four days out, and then only buried me in paperwork. The expectation was that I continue my role, despite what they had heard. Incredible. I was a nervous wreck—constantly suffering panic attacks, anxiety flooding my every cell around the clock. I needed to confide in someone, but who? It was so fucked up, and not to mention illegal, that I was put off by HR."

She told him, "The shame of what had happened made me want to hide and talk to no one. It was incredibly hard to share the news with my fiancé, who was then stationed in Paris. The hours ticked by and I reached out to my closest friends and told them what had happened. One of them immediately referred me to a forensic psychologist, who then guided me to make official reports to the authorities and such. I tried desperately to hide my pain from my son but failed miserably. The worst part was having to go back into that office, every single day, and pretend as if nothing had happened in front of my other 500+ colleagues and professionals on site at HQ.

"I used to be the open girl with a ready smile and grateful outlook. Not anymore. That shift in my persona was palpable—drawing the inevitable looks and concerned questions. 'Are you alright? Is everything okay?' The canned, automatic societal lies were programmed to say in return felt like shards of jagged glass in my throat. With each swallow and fake attempt to assure them I was business as usual I was sure they could see inside me, the blood draining from my face, trickling down the tiny raw slices in my throat. So, naturally, I let all my friendships with my colleagues go. It was an act of self-preservation.

"Two weeks after the attack, I flew to New York to attend the Women of the Channel East conference in New York City. It was a huge honor to be invited to such a junior role, and it was testament to my performance and abilities as a young tech writer. Not only did I attend, all expenses paid for, but I had a private driver for my entire five day stay. Anyone who knows New York City will tell you what a perk this was, in 15-degree, icy cold, snowy weather.

"Speakers at the conference touched upon the "Me Too" movement, which at then had just begun to break. I wanted to die and crawl into a hole. Here I was surrounded by these amazing and powerful women, in possibly the safest space I could have been in. And still, I couldn't find my voice to raise and tell even a total stranger what had happened to me just two weeks before. I was stuck in this ballroom, wearing the Big Global lanyard around my neck feeling the weight of it like a for-profit prison industrial complex proverbial ball and chain.

"I was sure these powerful women could see I was an imposter. The empowering experience I had been looking forward to was ruined. I left the sessions early, numb from my pain, and found myself walking aimlessly through the cold and windy New York streets. I ended up at the infamous Christmas tree in Rockefeller Center, surrounded by the magnificent windows all cheerfully displaying a life that I could never have.

"My son had asked me to please, please, pretty please visit the Pokémon World Center and film the experience for him on my iPhone. I ended up in this clean, modern, and colorful store, wanting to buy him some rare plushies as holiday presents, but just wasn't in the spirit and kept worrying about hanging onto every penny coming in. The ominous dark shadow of Big Global's brutal attack was slowly seeping into every corner of my life. First my showers and now the Pokémon store. This had to stop.

"I left New York, but not without my boss calling me from India, at all hours of the day and night, wanting to talk. In the bath, in the car, in the conference sessions, in the toilet, calling, calling, calling me. I ignored his calls, which felt like an act of rebellion, when in fact it was only an act of terror. I was terrified to speak with him and couldn't imagine his audacity. Disgusting tiny tech dick pig fuck.

"I flew home from New York, back to California on the red eye, and got back into the office the next day. I had to prepare to depart for another conference in Chicago that was coming up. The Chicago conference came and went, with nothing remarkable to report. I had an early flight back and found myself in the empty 4:00 a.m. hotel lobby with a colleague who was flying back to Texas from the same airport. We decided to split an Uber to the airport and discovered our flights left from the same terminal and airline, so our gates were near each other… Once we were past security, we decided to grab some breakfast at Dunkin Donuts together before our flights.

"When we sat down, I respected this man . . . but by the time my coffee was gone, so was my appetite and my respect for him. We began talking about Big Global's Corporate Social Responsibility Initiatives. I liked the concept but was concerned about their execution. There had been rumors in the corporate world about little orphan Ugandans in grass huts being exploited as they paid to win bogus awards like "Top Employer of the Year" and "Best Women in the Workplace Environment," when in reality, the rumors I heard, if true, sent a terrifying shiver down my spine.

"As he tore into his breakfast sandwich, I asked him if he had heard about the whispers that the single mothers and vulnerable minority women who had been recruited for our CSR cybersecurity level one training rehabilitation hadn't been treated fairly. He confirmed by nodding his head up and down as he chewed half the sandwich in one bite. Once he was clear, he said he had. He said, 'In fact, I was there. It was a shame what he did.'

'What who did?' I asked. Then he said, while inhaling the rest of his sandwich, Oh! I thought you'd heard! The man instructing that graduating class was busted for forcing unwanted sexual relations with most of the women in that class.' I was shocked. The blood drained completely from my face and I responded, Excuse me? Are you telling me that every woman in the class was raped by that man? What happened to the women? What services were provided to them? Where are they now?' He just said, 'What do you mean, what did we do for them? We gave them jobs!"

"Stunned, I got up and walked away in silence. I managed to make it into the women's restroom and into a stall before I puked. I flushed the toilet and put my laptop bag over the toilet and sat on it. *Fuck it*, I thought. I couldn't believe that the powerful men of Big Global would stoop so low as to prey on vulnerable single mothers, with multiple kids, trying to earn a better living for themselves. That program was supposed to offer them a glimmer of hope—taking them from $8.00 an hour jobs to $80,000 in just one year, then placing them with full time jobs with major companies. But it was all a lie. All of it. And they bragged on LinkedIn and Facebook, congratulating each other for a job well done, when by "job" they meant that they preyed on vulnerable women and took advantage of them. They raped them in the worst way. Beyond the physical violence and violation—no, no what they were doing was far worse. They were dangling low hanging fruits and playing on these women's drive to provide and do right by their children. This—this was the greatest violation of all. To make them feel that somehow, they may just have to endure and allow this vile behavior to play itself out, so that they may keep their jobs. No. This was unacceptable. This went too far. This was just how I felt—cornered. Like, was I supposed to play along? If I didn't say anything . . . I might get to keep my job. But if I called the police and filed that report, if I told the truth, if I did the right thing, they would take away my lifeline. And that right there was what made me dig my feet in real deep as I swore to myself that I would get justice, and blow that mother fucking emergency whistle for myself and for all the women they had done this too. Uh-uh. NO more. I was about to show them just how tough a girl from Inglewood could be. Believe that.

"So, I heard my name on the loudspeaker being called to board. I quickly got up and flushed the toilet again, ran to the sink, and washed my hands and rinsed my mouth out with some water from the faucet. I pulled a long sip of water from my water bottle, picked up my carry-on, and ran like hell for the gate. The brutality of his words lingered like a bad dream, echoing in my head. "What do you mean, what did we do for them? We gave them jobs . . . "Holy shit. This was bad. I just had to make my flight and get back to HQ. At this point I knew I had to return to the head corporate office and see if I could help myself and help all those women.

"It was a long flight back home, trying to calm my busy mind, but I was livid. As I sat in that privileged extra comfort seat, I thought about how just like that, my life was about to change. There would be no more glamorous international flights with drivers to meet me. Come to think of it, I would have to seriously consider whether or not to keep the upcoming Mumbai, Singapore, and Malaysia meetings. No more domestic travel, two phones, and two lightweight laptops to juggle. All of it meant nothing to me anymore. Absolutely nothing at all in comparison to my wellbeing, the safety and wellbeing of my son, and helping myself and those women who felt that they had no voice.

"As I sat there, I tried to find something in all of this to be grateful for. Knowing full well that the universe plays its hand in mysterious ways, and that quite possibly on the other side of this major life roadblock, I thought it just might be trying to reroute me to a better final destination. This left me with a *Now what?* nagging at me as I realized this meant I was about to journey deep within. My life was deep in the heart of Silicon Valley now. After everything, I'd gotten a contract with a biotech start-up in Santa Clara that allowed me to work remotely and fly up bi-weekly to collaborate, and I felt damn lucky to have found work after exhausting my unemployment while feeling paralyzed by the trauma Big Global had inflicted upon me. I felt angry and more than anything, I want justice and revenge. I just want to emerge safely on the other side, having my sanity, my health, and my spirituality intact. They're guilty, every single one of them, and I'm coming for them. I'm going to find them, hold them accountable for their actions, and make them pay."

CHAPTER TWO

Chocolat Chaud

A s she sat there, stuck on the plane, she thought about just how much they had taken away from her, and how only months before she was able to finally take her son to Europe, as she combined their holiday with a work trip. They had flown into Paris intending to stay in Tours, in the French countryside of the Loire Valley with her dear friend Marie, for over a month. They were able to leave their luggage at the farm and travel together all over Spain and France by train. They sat together in silence, watching the vibrant green countryside glide by their windows, as the steady rocking of the train lulled them into deep meditative states as it delivered them safely to Bordeaux, Toulouse, Nice, Monte Carlo, Barcelona, Madrid, San Sebastian, and finally Paris again.

The girl loved western European culture, from the architecture and cobblestone streets to its majestic churches, rich history, unfamiliar languages, and new and exciting foods. She wanted to breathe all of it in while getting lost walking down unfamiliar alleys whose window shutters were painted in bright blues and reds, giving life to ordinary spaces. There was beauty everywhere here, she thought, and hoped her son agreed.

She remembered their last day together in Paris before they would head to the UK where she would work from her London office for a week. That last day she woke up the boy early and wanted to cram as much "true living" as possible into their final 24 hours in her heart's favorite city of light. They began in the 19th arrondissement at the café some six steep and narrow flights below their hotel room some six steep and narrow flights above. She loved how, after only a week, her son was able to order his "chocolat chaud" in French, and she admired the service as their regular waiter (impressed by the American boy's effort) remembered their order and delivered excellent service with an approving wink.

From there, they caught the metro to the Louvre de Rivoli exit as they made their way to the Louvre. They took silly pictures outside the iconic sacred glass geometry above, before making their way down into the labyrinth of art and treasures below. The boy loved it all, taking selfies with the Mona Lisa as he wiggled his way to the front of the crowd. They walked and talked for hours, finally taking a well-deserved break in a terrace café, sharing a chocolate tart with some water for him and a glass of pinot noir for her. The café there was packed and the only seating available was outside, behind a gargoyle, on a rare grey cloudy day in late August. As they sat down to enjoy their treats, the skies opened up with light summer showers. Yet, they didn't mind; instead, like all those around them, they were happy for the moment, feeling grateful for a place to sit and rest their legs.

She checked her phone and looked at the time. It was already five p.m.! Where had the day gone! Shit, she thought—she still wanted to show him the Jardins de Luxembourg. They decided they had done the Louvre properly and decided to leave after their snack. This part she remembered, because it was one of the only times she had ever lied to her son.

"Mom, I'm really tired and my legs hurt from all the walking. Can we go home?" he asked.

By "home he meant the hotel, but she knew just what he meant.

"Sure honey, that sounds like a plan," she said. And that was it. That was the lie. For she knew the city well, having traveled there often since she was a girl, and even lived there once in her twenties.

So, she led them back down to the Metro, and jumped onto the line 2, exiting to the gardens. The boy was tired; she felt a little bad as she looked at the way he was dragging his feet. But she thought *you're only in Paris once* and wanted to show him some of her favorite, most magical places in the city. They had done Pere Lachaise, Montmartre, the Tour de Eiffel, Les Island Secret, and everything in-between. The garden was last on her must list for him. As soon as they arrived back up at street level, the boy looked around at a demonstration gathered around the exit and knew what she had done.

"Mom! You promised!!!" She felt bad for just a second.

"Yes, but *look* honey! Just look at all of this! And you might never get the chance to come back! I just couldn't let you go back up to the room without seeing all this! Come on, love—let's go sit and you can rest on the grass."

"Fine!" he said, clearly pissed with her.

"But I get to use your work phone and play games!" he spat.

What could she do? They found a place in the open wide green lawns and the boy laid his tired head in her lap and pulled his hoodie up over his head, making a makeshift gaming tent.

She took a green apple from her bag and the small wine opener she always traveled with and began cutting little slices from the apple with the small knife at the end.

"Ewwww!" she said as she spat the half-chewed bitter pulp out onto the grass.

"Bad apple, mom? Maybe that's your karma?" said her son.

"C'est une blague!" she returned.

"Did I ever tell you what my nickname was when I lived here?" she asked. "It was 'crasher de feu!'" she offered, not waiting for his response.

"Ugh, yes mom, like a million times when we were at Montmartre where you used to live. I know, I know, back when you used to skate still and would rap and hang out on the streets with your friends and grind down the steep inclines and they called you spit fire like the skate stickers on my deck. See? I listen," said her son.

So, he did. She was impressed and was about to say so when the sky opened up in a downpour. They scrambled up and ran across the field toward the metro playing an impromptu game of soccer with her apple. When they descended the stairs, back down under the city, into the maze of tunnels below the earth, he made her promise they were, in fact, returning to their actual hotel, and if not, she would owe him a hundred dollars. Feeling tired herself, she agreed and began looking forward to another last glass of wine and a cigarette in the piano bar next to their café.

So French.

He was too tired to be disappointed that he had not won the bet. Instead, he asked her for a key to the room before the long walk up to the penthouse suite.

"But aren't you hungry, my love?" she asked of him.

"No, I just want to go lay down on my bed and watch videos. Just bring me anything you feel like when you're done." And with that, the tired boy disappeared into the lobby, leaving her free to go sit and enjoy her last few moments alone in Paris.

The café was crowded, but she managed to find a seat outside at a small bistro table. Packed.

She ordered a glass of red wine and water from the waitress and took out her phone to look through all the pictures they had taken today. She reached into her bag and fished for the packet of cigarettes and some matches. She lit up, inhaled and exhaled deeply, leaning her long neck and chin up toward the sky.

She raised her glass to her full lips and took a long sip of the wine. As she lowered her glass, she took a moment to look around her at all the bustling activity on the streets before her. She loved the 19th for all its cultural diversity, bright colors, and motion. She thought to herself, *you could sit on this street for hours and be content just observing the life flow unfolding all around her.*

It was then that she saw him. A beautiful man, standing with 50 other people at the bus stop to Gambetta. He had earbuds in and was listening to music as their eyes connected for the first time. Their eyes locked for just the briefest of moments, and she felt an almost supernatural jolt, just as his face broke open into the most exquisitely beautiful smile she had ever seen. His skin was the blackest black, smooth against his chic light blue summer suit. His dark complexion made his perfect white smile, and those full lips reach her with the strength of a thousand hellos. Startled, she realized she had been staring and quickly became self-conscious, shifting her gaze out onto the street directly in front of her.

What a strikingly beautiful man, she thought as she turned her head toward the bus stop to her left again—she just had to look back! There he was, standing steady, enjoying his music, still smiling back at her.

Why . . . she was flirting with him! This was very unlike her, and with a stranger at a bus stop! Unheard of, as she moved through life with her erogenous switch permanently flipped to "off" mode, as so many single parents do. Still, their attraction was undeniable. It was as if she saw a ray of light energy surrounding him. His smile was ethereal. If it wasn't for the bus approaching in the distance . . . THE BUS! They continued to play this intimate game of eye tag as the bus rolled in from the east, but the bus had arrived! Oh, this was too much—she couldn't watch. If he got on, she would never see him again. She snuck glances toward him as he appeared to be a gentleman, letting all the people around him board before he did. But as the numbers dwindled, she just couldn't watch, so instead she picked up her wine glass, looking straight ahead out onto the street, and took a sip. She reminded herself to breathe, having realized she had been holding in her stomach. She saw the Gambetta line creep slowly into her line of sight from the left and pass her by. She took another deep breath and counted slowly to three. Then she turned her head back to the spot where, just moments before, he had stood.

The sky cracked with thunder and as she drew her eyes to the bus stop, the beautiful man standing there with an even bigger smile on his face and his tall regal posture, as he threw his arms out in a gesture as if to say "Ta-Da! Here I am!" He took long strides toward her on the crowded street, approached her table, leaned over, and asked if he could take a café with her.

She said yes, and they sat together, the man taking his café, as she slowly sipped her wine. They quickly discovered many things about one another. She had exhausted her best French after ten minutes and casually slipped into English, which he was able to reciprocate. Suddenly, the sky overhead broke, releasing another rare torrential summer downpour. He asked if he could scoot in closer to her, as his chair left him just outside the protection of the café's awning.

Hundreds of tiny metal chairs scraping concrete sounded little chirps into the air as people everywhere did the same. On the street, people ran under awnings and drew coats and bags up over their heads or ran for cover. They were drawn closer by the storm, their eyes soft, the heat between them palpable. He suggested they move inside, out of the storm. She agreed and as they stood up, she had a flicker of panic as she thought a silent prayer, *Please let him be taller than me*, and they ran into the café and up to the bar.

She drew up to her full height, 5'11," and thanked all the Gods in silence and shared her most beautiful smile with him as he revealed himself to be a perfect 6'2" indeed. They made their way into the bar and stood against the rich dark paneling.

"Où est tu parapluie? Where is your umbrella?" he asked in his beautiful French-African accent.

"J'en ai pas une parapluie! I don't have an umbrella," she said as she laughed, thinking about the long adventure this day had been.

"You must not go—please stay right here—I will return for you," he said very seriously. Then, he left and dashed out into the rain and down the street toward the shops—away from her, lifting his blazer up over his head as he ran down the street and out of her sight.

She really had no idea where he had gone to and was rather captivated by it all. She reached for her phone to call her son and check in. He answered on the fifth ring with the voice of a kid who was preoccupied by the screen before them.

"Hi Mom, . . ." came the slow video-distracted drawl.

"Hi love . . . I just wanted to check on you. I'm still in the café—is everything alright? Did you see the rain?"

"Mmmmmm yeah, sure," he said from a million miles away.

"Listen, I'm down to 2%—I thought I'd stop and bring in Chinois from that spot on the corner. How does that sound?"

"Mmmm sure, whatever . . ." came the little voice.

"Okay, just tell me, are you small, medium, or large hungry?"

"Medium, thanks Mom."

"You're welcome sweetheart, see you in a few."

She hung up the phone just as the man returned, filling the doorway with his presence, and walked quickly over to her. He stood before her with a look of pride as he held out the most beautiful umbrella that she had ever seen. It was perfect in a way that she had never known existed for an umbrella. It was old-timey, with a full erect long shape, all black, except for a cherry wood u-shaped handle. The trim on the piping of the fabric was enclosed with a light beige fabric that perfectly suited the piece.

"Voila!" said the man as he held out the umbrella to her.

"Now you have an umbrella, and you are safe," he said in broken English.

The girl quickly thought of what this umbrella signified, as she had never, ever received an umbrella as a gift from a man before. It represents protection from the elements, she thought. It was a kind and caring act. It was thoughtful of the man, and she was delighted.

Chill downtempo music floated up from behind the bar and they began to sway their hips to the music softly. Each smiling, they continued chatting, him learning that she would leave Paris again in the morning and head to England for work. She also had two return tickets for Paris next week but wanted to see where this went first. The man looked sad at this news, and they exchanged emails and cards with the intent to stay in touch. She wanted to get some food for the boy before the corner shop closed for the night, so he paid their bill and they stepped out onto the street together. Still smiling, he walked her past the bus stop where they had met from afar just moments before and walked her past the Metro entrance and to the corner. Just a very light rain fell now, as they leaned in and brushed their lips together in a petal soft kiss. Then came the embrace, side to side, cheek to cheek, and slowly, they pulled away.

He left her there on the street as he turned and disappeared, descending the stairs to go wherever it was he was going. She turned and waited for the light, then crossed the street with her new umbrella in one hand and opened the door to the Chinese shop. A tiny shop bell rang as the door opened and she approached the counter and began a to-go order. She walked back across the street, entered their hotel, and began the long steep seven-floor climb to their small room overlooking the streets below.

Her son lay on the bed, with his phone clutched tightly in both hands, his eyes weary from screen time. She took in the smattering of light freckles across the bridge of his nose and the natural blond highlights in his thick curly brown hair and thought about how quickly he was growing up. He had thick leg hair coming in, an indication of the man he was becoming. But there was more. This one held a deep calm power within himself, and one day, should he choose it, he would become a powerful shaman. He was capable of so much, in so many different realms. She could sense it.

Tomorrow in London, they would get a call that would shift his young life too. A coveted Montessori charter school he was on the waitlist for would ring them with an immediate opening. In order for him to reserve his seat in the class, he would end up flying halfway around the world, by himself. With no parent, no guide, just his good sense, upbringing, manners, logic, and faith to guide him. No cell phone, no unaccompanied minor service—just one small boy on a journey to begin the sixth grade at a new middle school. His grandfather Bubba would be there on the other side in Los Angeles to pick him up from the Tom Bradley International Terminal. Of all people to search, immigration would pull the young boy aside and search his bag, delaying him some two hours, causing Bubba some concern. But would be well, and despite being jet lagged, when he is dropped off in front of the school the next morning by Bubba, he would be ready to face the school all on his own.

"Naw, I'm good. I think if I can navigate a flight halfway around the world on my own, I can find a sixth-grade classroom door." As he jumps out of the car, he would give a casual wave and turn to walk the other way, presumably toward the right doorway. He would make it, and for years to come would say, "I think I can handle it, Mom. Remember London?"

London was a blur of fast-moving pink taxis, pubs, more pubs, curry, art, long walks among bright green fields with friends, shopping, and massive oversized breakfast buffets that were included with the room. Eggs, giant sausages, roasted tomatoes, and baked beans with bread and jam were popular here but were not her cuppa.

Her friend Dazzles came up from Bristol to crash on their pull-out sofa and spend a couple days showing them around the city. He was a cardboard artist and one of her favorite friends on social media. She liked him well enough but was a little disappointed to learn he wanted something more, something she just wasn't willing to give him. So, they made the most of their time walking and talking, dodging downpours, each trying to fill the silences. She was clear with him about the man she had met back in Paris, but sensed the envy lingering behind his polite facade.

London was London, and she couldn't wait to get back to Paris. She had been on WhatsApp with the man from Paris all week. They had been making plans for her return, and each day she fantasized just a little about what might be. On the morning she took her son to Heathrow International Airport, she almost forgot her umbrella at the hotel. She navigated their way on the train to the airport, got through the queue to the ticketing agent only to learn that in England, the airlines did not offer unaccompanied minor services. You either knew your kid was mature and respectful enough to make the flight and reach their destination on the other side or you just didn't put them on the plane. Her son stood at the counter pleading with her to let him go.

"Mom! I've got this! You've done a really good job teaching me how to be good in the world. What's the point if I don't ever get to use it?" he said loud enough for all 50 people in earshot to cast him sympathetic glances.

"The boy's got a point," said the Virgin ticket agent.

"True, but you don't even have a cell phone! How will I know if you've made your flight? What if I say yes, and take my train back to France, only to learn that you're stuck here in London hours later? This is hard for me. Really hard," the girl said, twisting her hair up and under her beanie.

"Please, Mom! I know I can make it! I promise! I will be good, and Bubba and I will call you from home when I make it there safe. Mom, please! You're going to have to let me go sometime," he pleaded.

"I know, but I'm not ready," she thought, biting her big bottom lip, thinking he'd made a fair point. "Let's say I believe in you. I believe that you can do this by yourself. But it's the other weirdos and whackos I worry about. Tell me, what would you do if you needed help or felt you were in trouble?"

"Easy. I would approach any airline employee in an official uniform and ask them for help, just like you taught me." He said, looking up at her with a confident smile.

Her heart was breaking—decisions, decisions.

"I'm afraid you're gonna have to make up yer mind, love. We've got to keep the line moving. Now, what would you like me to do about the boy's ticket?" the agent asked, looking annoyed.

"Can I walk him to the gate?"

"Security only, Mum. Sorry," came the reply.

So, it was with a heavy heart that the girl took out her credit card and handed it to the agent. One direct flight to LAX on the 11:11 a.m. flight today, please.

"Yes!! Mom, you're the best! I promise I'll make it okay! You'll see!" he said as he threw his arms around her in a long, hard hug.

The people all around clapped and the agent began typing furiously, producing the boy's ticket way too quickly. They walked to the security gate as she rattled off a plan, random security tips, and any other overprotective/worrisome nervous "Mom" thoughts that she couldn't stop herself from oversharing.

"Ugh! I've got it Mom! Trust me! I promise, pinky promise, I've got this!" he pleaded.

"Fine. Here's 20 pounds. This is enough for you to get some snack foods and water, do *not* get soda, on the other side for your flight. Do you hear me? They will serve you a meal and provide free drinks and have snacks for you on the plane too. Okay?"

"K, Mom. A thousand times, I've got this. Jeeze."

"Honey, I just love you so so much, and if anything happened to you, I don't know what I would do with myself. You are my heart, my soul, my world. You know that. Please be safe and call me as soon as you are with Bubba, alright? Promise Mommy you will see me safe on the other side real soon, okay?" she said with tears in her eyes.

"I promise Mom, I love you too."

"Alright then, here is your passport and boarding ticket. This is your gate number. When you get past security and you put your shoes back on and get your backpack, be sure to put this inside in a safe place. Follow the signs. Look up and follow the signs to your gate. Listen to the announcements and be brave. Don't talk to anybody, you hear me?"

"Alright, Mom. Alright. I love you," he said, looking past her toward the line.

"I love you too, honey. So much. Go on, then. Go make Mommy proud and get to your new first day of school, okay? Tell Bubba I love him too."

"I will, Mom."

And with that, the boy turned away, ticket in hand, and headed toward the TSA line and his independence.

She was a mess. She stood there and watched him go through security all the way down, watched him putting his shoes back on, then his hoodie, and messing with his backpack. She was waving to him, but he was already in his own world. She stood there until she couldn't see him any longer, then she ran out of the airport and walked briskly to the train station with tears streaming down her face. She hoped she had done the right thing.

Her journey was just beginning again. Her first train from Heathrow to Victoria Station took longer than expected, putting her in a mad dash for the underground train to Paris. The silver lining was that in all her rushing, she didn't have time to hyper-focus on the boy's journey. She silently prayed and asked her ancestors to be with him and guide him well. She made her train and found her seat just as the train pulled out of the station, when she got a text notification that her son's flight had been delayed.

"Shit! Now what?" she muttered aloud.

"Fuck, fuck, FUCK!"

She closed her eyes, as there was nothing she could do now, and prayed all would resolve by the time she reached Gare du Nord station in Paris.

An hour went by, when she received a second alert that there had been a gate change.

It was all of her fears coming true. Beside herself with worry, she got up to pee.

Once inside the small bathroom, she sat on the toilet, facing the mirror, and there behind her, smiling down upon her, was the campy smiley version of the Mona Lisa. Immediately, she knew that her son had made it and would arrive just fine. Just last week at the Louvre, he had been obsessed with the original Mona Lisa painting and took hundreds of selfies while she waited for him outside on a chair. She knew this was the universe's way of letting her know he had made his flight. What's more, when she finished, flushed the toilet, and stood up to wash her hands, there on the subway tiles were two daisies painted in connecting arches. Her favorite flower was a daisy and the girl believed nothing happened by accident. Feeling greatly relieved, she returned to her seat and began to look forward in earnest to her adventures in Paris.

She had returned to Paris to see the man again. She called her lifelong friend Jean-Francois (who happened to work for the French army in cybersecurity) to tell him what she was up to and where she would be staying. It never hurt to be too smart or careful and stay one step ahead. Besides, what if he turned out to be a maniac? And besides, the man from the bus stop would never know.

She was nervous and excited to see him as her underwater TGV train pulled into Gare du Nord station. In her head, she had visions of him waiting for her on the train platform, a bouquet of flowers in hand. But he was nowhere in sight. As she stood there, looking around, rolling her bag behind her, she thought of all she had shifted to be here with him, and he didn't have the courtesy to meet her train. Not a good sign. She stood with her purse, suitcase, and the umbrella, waiting a fair amount of time, long enough for the trains to be empty as the cleaning crews boarded and police with large semi-automatic rifles walked around and around, securing the area.

She tried to call him but got no answer. She sent an email and waited. She walked outside into the evening twilight and scoped out the area. It was a little sketchy even by her measures in front of the station, and she decided to keep moving and not stand still here, looking like an easy tourist target.

She saw a busy café on the corner across the street past the taxi zones and headed there. There was one spot open facing the street, and she barely managed to squeeze her luggage under the table as she took a seat at the small round table. The café was bustling. Two businessmen sat to her left drinking rosé and smoking cigarettes. Eventually, the waiter came, and she ordered a glass of red wine, some water for the table, and gave him instructions to bring out an espresso for the man, when he joined her.

"Oui madame," said the waiter as he disappeared.

He returned to the table delivering a happy hour special: two tapas bowls, one filled with an assortment of olives, the other with some dry nuts. Her phone rang and it was the man calling to say he apologized but his work demanded his presence and that he was en route to Gare du Nord, but with apologies, and obviously late.

"Pas du problème," she said, wishing she knew how to say "I noticed" instead. She gave him the name of the café on the corner and hung up the phone. She sat there watching people, listening to the conversations flow around her, checking her emails, and enjoying the early September night.

When he finally arrived, she observed the same intense chemistry between them, despite being less than thrilled with the last 40 minutes and imprint of disappointment. She chose to ignore the slight stares from the two Frenchmen next to her. Having long been out of fucks for such ignorance, she channeled her attention to the arrival of his café and took joy in the surprised face of the man.

"But how did the waiter know I will take a café?" he asked with surprise, in that beautiful, accented French African-English.

"I told him to bring you one when you arrived," she said and smiled at him.

It was a beautiful beginning. The loving energy that surrounded them was evident. These two would dance and fly, court and walk, fuck, run, taste, smell, cry, care, caress, massage, and love one another fiercely for the next couple of years. He would stand by her side, during her best and worst times. He would send her money when she needed to cover attorney fees, upfront. He would listen wisely to her as her nerves took her on a wild ride. He would send his love and gifts to her and the boy from Paris. He would pray the strong Muslim prayers and protect her and her son, so many miles away in California. He would be her savior in many, many tiny ways until the ordeal was complete. But that is another story . . .

What was relevant now was this deep love affair personified every Sade song in existence. It was an "It's Only Love That Gets You Through" meets "By Your Side" kind of love. Theirs was a "Love is Stronger Than Pride" and" No Ordinary Love" love. It was as magical as *Sleepless in Seattle*, but also tragic in a new postmodern way. Meeting the man changed everything for her and allowed her to focus on healing and growing herself in every single way that mattered most.

In fact, nothing would ever be the same in her life again.

The plane began its final descent into San Jose bringing her back to work at Biome. The girl was deep in the heart of the Silicon Valley now, she was angry, and more than anything, she wanted justice. The girl wanted to emerge safely on the other side, having her sanity, health, and spirituality intact. She was coming for them. She was going to find them, hold them accountable for their actions. After all . . . they took away Paris.

CHAPTER THREE

Fuck This Shit

On a winter day, she surfaced, focused on her mission to survive, thrive, and be alive. There were two things on her mind this morning: the haunting memory of the rape still swirling around in her brain, filling her natural light aura with inescapable dark shadow work, and the fact that Djedi was not by her side. These two triggers cast shadows over her natural light, blocking her magic. It was almost February again, which meant it was almost a year since he proposed to her on that snowy winter night in Paris. A lifetime ago now, she thought to herself as she gazed out of her Silicon Valley office window and allowed herself to remember the last time, she had seen him in the city of light.

As she stared out the window, she thought back to when she had first met him. She had been traveling back to the EU every quarter for work, tagging on extra days in the city to be with him. It was fucking freezing this time out—colder than even the winter of '97 in Paris when she could only afford to dry her thermals in the laundromat and had to wear her damp overalls over them, trudging through the snowy banks along the Seine until she could finish work, get back home, and hang them over the furnace to dry in her tiny shared seventh-floor studio apartment in Montmartre.

Joyfully reunited, the happy couple returned to their favorite hotel on the corner of Rue des Pyrénées and Arnaud Saint in the 19th. They liked it because it was a studio with a complete kitchen which allowed them to playhouse together, saving money and creating intimacy simultaneously. They knew the people who ran the hotel by name now and were considered favored guests. So here they were again, as she tried to adjust yet again to being catapulted nine hours forward. Her eyes were still puffy from the alcohol on the plane, but he was kind and did not mention this. Instead, he asked if she wanted to head to Indian Alley, otherwise known as Brady Passage, for dinner with him. She said she was too tired, so they made do with some take away sandwiches from the café below instead and fell asleep wrapped safely in each other's arms, united in a deep and long winter night's sleep.

The next day, they rose with the sun. This was one of her gifts—the one that allowed her to travel as she did. No matter the time zone, she could always rise with the sun. The first light showed her more snow out below on the streets than she had ever seen in her beloved city of grey—white lights dancing below to the whispering icy winds. She ran through her head what she had brought to wear and realized she was grossly unprepared.

Hearing her concerns as they grabbed a quick café in the café downstairs, he decided to take her to a part of the city where old secondhand shops may be able to help to solve her (now their) dilemma.

The shops did not disappoint. She found a large grey winter coat from the late '70s, made from some kind of weatherproofed suede with a thick sheepskin lining. It had a long grey rope belt that tied around her and kept all the warmth in. She instantly loved it and felt that the 33-euro price made it even better. They picked up some gloves for her and a few other souvenirs from a chic vintage shop. Memoirs. Memories. Memories of walking arm in arm with him, all bundled up, searching for his uncle's African magic shop.

Bright blue and green paint jumped out from the building where his tiny alchemy studio ran. There were already four people ahead of them, all sitting on makeshift chairs, waiting for the uncle to mix a potion, tonic, or brew for them. People would walk in, announce their ailment, and the uncle would disappear into the back behind a patterned curtain of tiny beads to mix the herbs that would ease their minds, soothe their spirits, and maybe even help their bodies too.

Uncle was a man of perhaps 65 with a medium build and a small, completely bald head. His eyes looked into you—searching for the truth. Looking at this man in the eye was no problem for the girl and she began to share with him what she was here for. She felt embarrassed to speak aloud in front of all these strangers in her broken French but leaned into it anyway.

"Bonjour mon oncle, je, je euh, je souffre de nerfs et je me sens souvent anxieux à l'intérieur. J'ai besoin d'aide pour gérer ça" (*Hello Uncle, I, I uh, I suffer from nerves and I am often feeling anxious inside. I need help managing this please*), she said bravely, in terrible but brave French, in front of everyone's curious ears.

Uncle ducked behind the curtain again and returned with some wood sticks and herbs and gave Djedi the words in their fast African dialect. Dejedi, in turn, patiently translated the instructions into English.

A ceremonial necklace on the wall jumped out to her—it hung from a wire hanger, a brilliant assembly of thousands of tiny red and yellow beads. It was built for a queen and she had to have it. She chose two larger white shell bracelets for her and her best friend Dilly and some more tiny copper-beaded bracelets to take back as souvenirs for her friends and their children.

She raised both her hands to her heart in prayer and bowed slightly, smiling as she thanked Uncle many times, sharing slow wide smiles back and forth as people with no verbal language to share often do. They left the tiny shop and stepped back out, huddling close together into the crippling cold.

Walking arm in arm down the street, they stopped in front of a bright flower shop, an anomaly in the snow. Seeing all those pretty bright colors on display set against the white backdrop was breathtaking. They walked the snow-covered streets aimlessly with no agenda, nowhere to be—just together and in the moment. If it weren't for the cold, they would have walked this neighborhood all day. But instead, he took her to a small restaurant near Saint-Michel where they sat intimately at a small table for two near the front windows. Tourists and locals alike wandered past them in the window at a frenzied pace. The restaurant was empty when they arrived, but full when they left, as the beautiful and exotic couple in the window surely raised some attention.

They took menus and he decided to order the chicken plate while she opted for a bowl of hot onion soup. It was their joke, that everywhere she went, the girl had to try their French onion soup, or soup d'onion. As usual, his chicken plate was better than her soup, and she eventually ended up eating half of his then ordering her own plate after.

There was magic about them being together. The small white candle lit in the center of their table cast its light into their eyes as they gazed at each other, smiled, and talked gently. Their conversation was filled with love and laughter as he mentioned marriage once again. This was not the first time he asked her to marry him—but it *was* the time that he had the ring for her.

He asked for both her hands across the table, gently folded them into his own, and asked her to marry him. "Be my wife, please, I cannot live without you" were his exact words. He then reached into his pocket and pulled out not one, but two thin golden rings. "Because today is Saint Valentine's day, my love," he said, reaching for her ring finger.

She had said yes months before on the phone, long distance. She jokingly said yes, the first time he asked, that first 72 hours they spent together. And for the third time, she said yes. "I will marry you Djedi." This made her the happiest girl in Paris that night. It was everything she had waited her entire life for: real true romantic love. This was it.

But what she didn't know—what she could not have possibly known—was that they would take all of this away from her. Big

Global not only fucked her when they fucked her, they crept in and sabotaged the most precious essence she possessed. Love. The night that Big Global raped and tortured her descended upon her, stealing her joy yet again, sentencing her to relive that brutal night in perpetuity . . .

A memory came to her: a memory of when the leaders of Big Global had lured her up into a '70s inspired bedroom with deep brown shag carpeting, a large orange velvet bedspread, and a massive painting of Jesus Christ hung above the center of the king-size bed upon the wall. Behind her was an inconsequential wooden mid-century modern dresser, a jar of Vaseline, and the fully erect but embarrassingly small penis of her manager, the CMO from London. He went first. Jamming and ramming his tiny tech penis into her anus again and again trading off with the rest of his C-Suite gang. Next was the CFO, followed by the CTO, the CIO, the CHO and finally the CEO. Vomit fell from her mouth and shit from her anus. Thick streams of bile and shit shot out of her, staining their ugly suits as the sisters swung. She passed out, thankfully; in-between the prayers, she screamed in her mind as she looked up into the face of Jesus on the cross. "Save me," she begged him. "If you're real and there really is a God, have mercy, please make it stop and save me now!" she cried to the painting and Judeo-Christian God above. Jagged snobby cries escaped her and rang out, startling the men. They moved in from behind again to tighten her gag. She fell into darkness, only to be awoken by some new level of physical torture as her body responded to them penetrating and violating her eight ways to Sunday. Grace came in waves when they would get spooked by a sound from outside and stop. That and the fact that the men from Kerala really did have the tiniest wee penises she had ever seen. These fragments of silence revived her as her spirit fought. She must have disconnected from the physical torture—the small perfect silver blade held around her neck barely nicking her corroded artery as the tip of the blade dug ever so slightly into the front of her throat. They beat her pretty face, kicked her in the kidneys, and whipped her ass from behind. One of them pulled her hair back and jerked her neck so swiftly, she thought for certain they would kill her. This was her introduction to corporate technology.

This was also the beginning of her spiritual growth and ultimate lifetime ascension through trauma and loss. Deep wounds required warrior, shamanic-level cures. Cures that no healthcare or western carrier could begin to wield or administer, respectfully. No—for this part of the journey she would have to journey deep into the thousand-year-old jungles. Brave the three levels of Shabalala and open herself one final time to rid herself of this cross she carried this lifetime. Once and for all, it had to happen, for there was no alternative—only death without rebirth.

Months passed by as the girl waited and waited to hear something back from her attorney. Anything. Her days were filled with long hours of numbing and hiding from the world.

She stood silent in her life, barely showing up for herself and listened for the way. Ancient forces deep within her stirred as she gradually began to remember a time when everything healed. The body healed. The heart healed. The mind healed. She was wise and believed in the spirit and that it would lead her to a time when joy and love and happiness would return to her life. The bad times would never last, but the strong person would. Lots of us were broken, but last time she checked, a broken crayon still colored. This wisdom was all but gone, just a dim glimmer in a jar below the earth. The girl laid her head down onto her pillows while lying on her bed. She was depressed and had been popping pills and day drinking again. As she drifted off into a light sleep, she was thinking about poor Mother Earth.

She began to dream and heal as Mother Earth came to her in the safety sublevels of consciousness that only REM sleep dreams provide. Mother Earth with all her exotic deep red clay dirt, magnificent complex oceans, and delicate flora and fauna began moving toward the girl. They were down, down below, far below the earth's surface, near the core in the place of the Masons where Mother Earth took the form of a woman vaguely resembling Maya Angelou, wearing a jockey cap made of global fabric while her ample curves were wrapped softly in a multicolored lush silk kimono. Underneath, she wore an old, faded pair of overalls and a simple white t-shirt, finished by a pair of hemp Adidas shoes, LavHa bracelets, and mandalas for days. Mother Earth was a pimp. Mother Earth was in us all.

As the girl looked around, she felt grateful to the many Masons around her for holding up hundreds of tiny jars filled with light, that it might be shared to light a thousand other candles back up above. Besides the Masons holding tiny Mason jars filled with soft glowing light, Mother Earth, and the girl, there was an entity of some sort, filling a white cloak lined with gold that was leading the way for her. This golden entity was called a "Shifter"—an angelic guide designed to help the girl safely defy dimensions and escape out of negative emotions with the ease of simply changing our moods.

Mother earth leaned into the girl and brushed the side of her face with her kimono, and whispered to the girl, "SO?"

"SO??? So, what," thought the girl.

"SO!" repeated Mother Earth, gently nodding her head up and down.

There was something about the way she said the word with just a hint of sarcasm that gave way to her wisdom and message.

"Ohhhhhh! SO!!!" said the girl again. In an instant, they both shared smiles and bowed deeply to one another, almost giggling with the power of SO.

Mother Earth made a funny voice and said, "I want this. I do not want that now. I will do this. I will not tolerate this anymore. I am not the culmination of all the vicious acts that have happened to me. I am a human being, not a human doing," and the like. The girl sat alone in the stillness, far below but never down, and listened to the strong voice guiding her, taking in the golden tones and the sage advice of Mother Earth and the power of SO.

Many moments had passed in silence, and the girl sensed that she was alone, once more within her dream. Mother Earth was gone, as were the Masons and her angelic Shifter too. Next to her on the ground were a pair of vintage Gucci glasses and a note written on the back of an SNCF metro pass from a Paris station on the 19th. The note said only this: HOMA. "HOMA?" she wondered out loud, breaking the silence of the Masons. "What is this HOMA?" she marveled. A quick glance around confirmed that her instinct was on point and, indeed, Mother Earth had moved on. The flame on her candle dipped feverishly low as she reached for the glasses, put them on, and felt guided to once again return to the surface above. Her triggers calmed and her inner scrappy quieted, she felt ready for what lay ahead and thus returned, ready to take the stairs back up, up, up, closer to the edge of her dream.

As she mumbled in her sleep, her body turned over, her head tossing from right to left on the pillow. Still in her dream, and now back above on the earth's surface, Father Time appeared to the girl. Father Time took the vague form of Samuel Jackson, if Samuel Jackson identified as a female pansexual boxer who could talk. Father Time revealed to her that the ultimate gift of healing lies within her. That the infinite wisdom as she spiraled amidst the deepest songs of sorrow would release all the pain, she carried within her, if only she could remember the key. She tried and tried to lock the key within her, but felt it keep slipping away.

Standing there next to Father Time, with the sensation of this key slipping away from her, she also felt as if she had downloaded insane amounts of divine data from him into her heart and mind. For example, she knew that all tragedies and miracles existed simultaneously within us, like a lotus flower harnessing the hope of all possibility within her. Designed, supremely to and for the exquisite colors of the masses. Names of groups flooded within her: The Rainbow Peasants, The Pharma's Victims, The Cunts, The Nepalese D'Balls, The Shandies, The Damned, The Regular, and The Elite alike. She raised her hand into the air before her and began scribbling symbols into the air in front of her. She was channeling ancient Akasha (she would later learn), transcribing the sacred texts while programming commands with the collective on an invisible hologram channel board, all by intuition.

Father Time watched her as he ruled all with an easy precision, answering only to a higher calling we would never understand (regardless of the plane of existence we subscribed too), ignorant of the intense prayers in our hearts. Ruthless in their own intelligent way, born with the power to stop life, precious life, in a moment and seemingly shatter our very existence. He ruled supreme, yet ultimately was the most compassionate guide we could ever wish for. Even when we were cruel to ourselves, Father Time's unlimited compassion and empathy blanketed us, forcing us to be gentle with ourselves until such a time had passed and we were capable of moving on, on our own.

Few knew that Father Time also carried the ultimate gift of compassion and empathy, always ready to watch over those suffering in his name, as he patiently guided them through the long, unforgivable processes of loss and grief. Like Mrs. Walker of Oakland, who had to learn that her son, her sweet baby boy, was the victim of a terrible and heinous botched robbery gone wrong at Morehouse College. That boy was brutally attacked and beat up, cut, and shoved into the back trunk of a car, only to have gasoline set upon him before being left there to die. Curled up with fear and fumes, his mama's intuition some 2,700 miles away sounded the alarms and got the policemen and the firemen out to make a wellness check on her boy, only to discover that her baby boy had been dead for some two weeks right under their noses. That unjust, inconceivable type of pain. They were born with this pain, having suffered at the beginning of tremendous trauma, and in the process of becoming, Father Time was every stage of despair that they had ever known. In a way, Father Time was our ever-present, omniscient angel. He made you feel - if only we could make it through every next moment trusting in blind faith that our lives would be, could be restored to a higher version of where we are now. A gifted shapeshifter, he took the form of whoever and whatever we needed to see, to purge, to let die within us, in order to make room for the next stage in our lives.

And this "next" was perhaps the most difficult part of all. For it called upon regular people. People without faith in their lives, without visions or callings to trust at that precise moment they felt taken advantage of, lost despite their pure best intentions, utterly un-magical, unremarkable, and not lit to completely trust and turn over the wheel. This was where and when Father Time came alive and let himself be known. Be known or drown. Choose wiser or succumb amid your weak attempts to mask the pain. Pain, (not bread in France, but actual pain), this pain was the arch enemy of Father Time and proved it time and time again. Everyone had their rapist—their darkest shadow manifested. Those who were among us, who in the name of some daily requirement known as survival we often have to let in. For some, this pain was a drink, or a smoke, or food. For others, exercise or sex. Pain was not announced with our polite introductions. Pain was a me-centric darkness that cared only for itself, damning all of us with every false start. This was the dream the girl experienced as pain and time first met the girl as she slept. It was only as Father Time slowly disappeared that the girl saw herself in the dream from above, as she saw herself lying below there, curled up on her side on her parents' shitty extra guest room bed, sleeping soundly, in the middle of the day with a half empty glass of red table wine next to her. A beautiful black and white long-haired cat was curled up next to her, watching over the girl as she slept.

When she finally woke up, she reached her hand out for the glass next to her. Her hand shook as she raised it to her lips and took a deep sip of the cheap red wine. She was but a fragment of her highest self on the day she drank the spirits, and after struggling with her decisions all day, she finally let her head fall upon the promised pillow to cry another jagged river alone. As the pull into darkness called her, she fought a battle deep within. Encouraged by her despair, pain hung around, filling her head with illusions, as the dark side hoped for a cheap victory. *No fucking way*, thought the girl. *For while I may be down, the spark of my instinct within still leads my way and I will not succumb to yours. Fucking loser pricks.* And just like that, the girl awoke not only from her daydreams but from her nightmare too.

The rape. If only she could forget about being raped. But it wasn't like that, was it? You just couldn't ever do normal shit and not completely lose it. Like seeing Vaseline. Her favorite non-fancy go to lip lubricant, now ruined for her. Or Jesus. There was no way she could see him on the cross without just a little vomit rising within her. In fact, Jesus on the cross triggered her so much, it provoked her to play a sick game of chicken with herself. She would think, "Okay, Jesus. If you're really real, and you died for our sins and blah, blah, blah, then why did you let that happen to me? Why do you let such shitty shit happen to innocent people all over this world? Why do you let six-year-old children receive books wrapped in cellophane to swipe right across their covers? Why let young girls in surf towns wear Ugg's with short shorts or miniskirts? What's the point? If you really want me to be alive right here, right now, then I'm going to jaywalk against this very fucking red light and not be hit by a car." So there! And off she would dart into the intersection. Still alive on the other side, she would shrug her shoulders and think... yeah, whatever. Easy Jesus. Big deal. But what she didn't know at this time was that it was God's miracles enabling her to push on despite the shitty evil things her energy attracted in the world.

Her phone buzzed with a message from a former colleague. That was strange. It said that they wanted to meet with her in the alleys of Kubit. She blinked away the salty tears gathered at the corners of her eyelashes from the remembering. It sucked that Big Global had brutally raped and discarded a loyal disabled girl. But it really sucked that they had been fostering this rape culture, preying on women for 17 years across four continents. They were professionals, alright—professional liars. They had promised her a promotion, set up meetings with leaders to confirm, and had made announcements company-wide and sent out corresponding encrypted emails. More meetings were held. HR was involved. More emails were sent. Dinners were had. Celebrations were, too. Then it all fell apart. They tried to destroy her career, kill her spirit, and fuck her good. No. They would pay. No longer would she take their shit, their ignorance, their prejudice, their sides, or their views. She laughed at their wants and needs and spat and kicked the red dirt earth upon anything presented as a want. For they were the guilty, the damned, and the greedy. They were the ones using and abusing to serve themselves. She would have their corpses hanging from cruel jagged posts nailed to the front of the disabled parking spots they stole. Their poor parking manners announcing to the world, "I SUCK BALLS, and have terrible ticky-tacky taste in automobiles as proven by my predictable Tesla." Telling us far more than their cheap analytic trackers could predict. In the worst possible way, the girl conjured up a spell and began to curse them right then, seven generations forward and back.

She wasn't sure what the outcome of this life experience would be, but at the very least, she would send each of her violator's a greeting card with, "Congratulations on your new STD!" That's right, you assholes, when you chose to rape her, you chose the whole enchilada. You now have HPV, so run and tell your wives and flings. Nothing says "'take that" like a gift that keeps on giving.

After another long day of hiding from the world, taking pain meds that couldn't begin to touch her pain while not living her best life, she fell asleep (as was her plan) to help the day pass faster. This dream began with a slot machine, number 10, with a payout of 77 times $10,000.00 and she held the hand that would have hit. *Well*, she thought, *gambling was never my thing*. Still, while reaching for her phone, a triangular group of shiny silver men shuffled toward her, resembling an old Del Taco commercial from the late '90s. A theme song accompanied their rhythmic shuffle as they approached the girl in unison. She felt something—not quite fear. She wasn't afraid; rather, an odd sense of bad familiarity came over her with the presence of this group. As their work boots scuffed against the linoleum floor, they came to an abrupt stop before her. These were the Tin Men, here to announce the coming of the Hackers. These Tin Men were the messengers of the Big corporate assholes who slashed, gashed, and willingly offended many in abuse of their power. The arrival of the Tin Men signaled to the girl the arrival of ominous times ahead. A fat dirty bird swooped out of the sky and dropped a sloppy turd onto the slot machine behind her. All eyes were on the girl as the music, noise, and action in the casino ground to a halt. The Tin Men all moved to reach into their back left pockets where their cell phones were. They pulled them out in choppy choreographed movements and pressed a button to open the DT App. There had only been whispers of this DT App back in the real world, a Digital Transformation App that could actually transform you digitally into the desired trending form of the entity behind the app initiation. The thing was, everyone talked about what this digital transformation was or looked like, but in reality, it didn't exist. It was a virtual hand job. And so, while slightly terrifying in concept, the app failed to launch, and the girl stood strong. Embarrassed by their epic fail, the Tin Men began their clumsy retreat, falling over one another as they moved away from her, eventually disappearing into the burgundy leather crowd. Cigarette smoke hung in a low casino haze and aging cocktail waitresses who called you "Honey" swarmed. The girl turned away from the machine and walked away, looking for an exit. As she walked down the rows of slots, they morphed into a computer lab, now resembling a Network Operation Center. In the heart of the NOC, tiny Hackers sat before each machine and monitored screens with a dead glaze and a sticky tacky pattern to their methodical typing. Large panel screens dropped down from the ceiling above, closing the girl where she stood.

Alone with the machines, these tiny Hackers, and the Ballad of Innovation playing over a surround sound system, the girl wondered to herself...where the fuck was, she? No sooner had she completed this thought, the ballad was interrupted as an Oz-like figure addressed her like Dorothy from behind the largest panel screen.

"YOU THERE," the big voice boomed!

"What's up, mutherfucker?" said the girl bravely.

"What did you say to me?"

"You heard me, you tiny tech dick prick. Come out from behind your fake ass innovative IP and talk to me like a man!" spat the girl.

"Surely you don't—" as the girl interrupted him.

"Oh, but I do! In fact, I am here to take your punk ass down. You see, the one thing you never counted on was the power of an independent woman's spirit. We are driven by love, faith, and passion. Our mantra is 'How you do anything is how you do everything.' Which means you are messing with a slew of 'do the right thing' women, and that makes us more powerful than you'll ever be. Now show yourself, you coward!" she yelled.

Silence.

"Your audible tracking software is going to fuck you in the ass," taunted the girl.

"It recorded everything you did to me. Everything. Your data is now my data. You're all finished," she said confidently.

Still, silence.

"I'm going to walk away now and you're going to let me. May the men of Kerala be eternally damned!" She raised her hands above her head and clapped them three times loudly as she spat onto the floor in front of her. A shrieking white hot silver scream pierced the air as the screens fell crashing to the floor.

The girl quickly awoke from this dream and reached for her phone. It was time to check in with her lawyer. Everyone wanted a "spiritual woman" until she was pissed off. Now she was a witch, and you were scared. *Well, fuck that*, she thought. Just because someone carried it well didn't mean wasn't not heavy. She was done carrying this alone. It was time to get down to business.

CHAPTER FOUR

New Pain

She was out on her morning walk when she heard a lady working with a young puppy, training him in French. He was a beautiful Great Dane who seemed to be named Rumi.

"Bon Marche Rumi!" sang the lady. He listened, was a good boy, and was rewarded with a cookie.

As the girl walked on by, the words "Mon Chérie, mon Coeur, mon amour toujours" flew out of *her* mouth, filling her heart with a deep sadness as tears welled up in her eyes. She had not said those words to anyone since the last time she had spoken to them on the phone to Djedi. Back when she still had a fiancé, was still very much in love, and her world had made sense. Saying the words now, to the dog, had happened so quickly, and she surprised herself with the volume of emotions they evoked within her.

The last year had been rough on them all, that's for sure. A cascade of memories flooded her—walking arm in arm with the love of her lifetimes, Djedi, along the Seine near St. Michel, taking silly pictures together along the bank at sunset. Attending the opening of the Islam & Africa exhibit at The Louvre with him thanking her for letting him "outside the box" that was his simple life. Remembering how they laughed when she took a moment and sat with the sketch artists before important works of art, pretending to draw—only to reveal herself portrait of two stick figures to him after several minutes of deep-fake-contemplation with just "LOL" staring back at them from her small journal. Sitting in cafés together, checking their phones, buying groceries in the store and cooking together, making love at 4:00 a.m. with the sound of the city coming to life outside as the rain fell lightly onto the rooftop windows above them.

The memories of her Paris with Djedi stirred deep within her, as it was all she had left of him. The night they raped her; they took more than they would ever know away from her. For they robbed her not only of her precious life's essence, shaving years off her life from the stress and panic they caused her heart all those days. No, worse still, they took away Paris. Beyond the haunting nightmares of physical torture was them stripping her of the greatest love she had ever known, while pushing her ten steps backwards and into the last place any grown ass woman wanted to be—back living with her parents at forty-something with a child in tow.

Fuckers.

It was 11:00 a.m. PST (7:00 p.m. in Paris) when she called Djedi to tell him about the rape. She remembered sitting cross-legged on top of the guest bed in her parents' house with the shades pulled as the long cross Atlantic-Euro elongated WhatsApp rings stretched out – beeeeeeeeeeeeep - beeeeeeeeeeeeep – before he finally picked up.

"Hello? Chérie? Ça Va?" said the strong sexy voice on the line.

"Oui, bonsoir mon amour toujours," she replied.

"Bon. Comment va-tu mon amour?" he inquired.

"J'ai – J'ai – J'ai quelque chose à te dire," she began, with an entire dam of sorrow behind her voice.

"Qu'est-ce qui ne vas pas mon amour?" he asked softly.

At this, the girl began to cry. That jagged, ugly cry scared him—the distance, stretching some seven-thousand miles across the globe, made moments like these almost too much to bear. Knowing he could do nothing but stay on the line and listen was his worst nightmare come true.

The man who had survived genocide in the diamond mines, who had fled not one but two regimes, lived on nothing in the jungle as a child with no shoes, had no formal education and no support system fell apart as he heard his fiancé tell him how she had been brutally attacked by her boss and his friends.

He was livid and saw white in ways only a black man can.

He bit down on his tongue so hard it bled. Still, he held space for her as she went on . . .

"I have something to tell you – and it is very difficult for me to talk about," she said in a strange voice.

"Continue," he said.

"You remember the night of my promotion dinner with my boss? Well, that night, after dinner, he walked me back to my car and tried to kiss me."

"D'accord. Continue chérie," he whispered.

"But the next night – the next night . . . they . . . they . . . they attacked me. They raped me, Djedi. They wanted to kill me, I'm sure." She lost it, wailing into the phone as he comforted her with a rush of kind words and his vows to be present and get her through this.

"What do you need from me right now?" her love asked her through tears.

She took some time to cry with him over the phone, and then began to share with him the details of her the night of the rape, filing the police report, going to HR, and then being wrongfully terminated just hours after she made her claims. The rotten bastards. She spoke with him about how she felt, how she was scared about her ability to pay her bills and rent, not to mention how was she going to swing everything now *and* hire an attorney?

He could feel her anxiety through the phone and begged her not to worry.

"Come to France—bring your son and stay with me here. We can be a family together! Pas de problème mon fiancé! Je t'aime tellement.," he offered.

The girl was silent.

"Do you need money? I can send you," he said.

She *did* need money but hated being in this position. But she also knew she needed to let him help her, and this was one small way he could feel that he was helping her. He cursed the current American administration for blacklisting all African nationals from his country. He was stuck and could not go to her. He was not there to protect her honor that terrible night, and so, he thought, the least he could do was send her some money to retain an attorney until they could assess the damage and make plans. He wanted to kill the men who had done this to her, yet he listened with a kindness and patience that few men possessed.

"I cannot take your money, my love," said the girl.

"But you will," he said firmly. "I will send you the western union confirmation code. I will go in the morning, when they open.

Does this mean you are not coming again in two weeks?" he asked.

"Yes, I'm afraid so," she replied.

She was a million miles away and fading fast. She had shifted to lie down on her side in a curled fetal position while they were talking. So many thoughts and things she was feeling; it was hard working with their limited French and English. Words scattered like thrips among plant leaves, aggravating an already bothered situation.

"You will stay with your family now?" he asked her.

"I don't really have a choice. I have to be here for the legal process and can't pull my son out of school when I'm falling apart. It's important to me that he has a stable and safe environment while I go through all of this. You understand, don't you?" she asked, hoping for a sympathetic response.

"Mais oui, chérie. Absolument. Je suis désolé mon amour. Très, très désolé," he soothed.

"Je prie pour que vous guérissiez des choses pour lesquelles personne ne s'est jamais excusé," he said, which meant "I pray you heal from things no one ever apologized for."

It was the kindest thing he had ever said to her.

They ended the call with the promise to speak again in several hours, as was their schedule. They each looked forward to the 8:00 a.m./8:00 p.m. zone, for it was when they were both able to connect and share some time with one another.

She was slowly coming to terms with the fact that while going to Paris with Dejedi was her happiness in this world, her first obligation was to her son who remained in California. With a mountain of credit card debt, no income, and a growing boy to look after and provide for, there was no way she could just duck out and justify abandoning her responsibilities. No. She was right where she needed to be. And now with legal issues to navigate, there would be no Paris for a while.

She felt horrible telling him like this, but he had to know. Life was difficult enough for her now and keeping a secret to herself—one of this magnitude—would have destroyed their trust and eventually been leaked in the end, or worse. Grief held within had a way of manifesting itself into undesirable disease that robbed you of life later. No, she needed to trust her instinct and continue on this journey to right this wrong that had been forced upon her. This was not her life. She wasn't sure what the universe had in store for her, but she was slowly learning to trust it. Was her faith returning? She certainly hoped so, as she silently vowed to remove the following things at the end of the day: bra, makeup, toxic people, and limiting beliefs. Head on, the girl thought. Head on.

CHAPTER FIVE
The Secret Sacred Balinese Women's Masterclass

Dilly was the girl's best friend and had been increasingly unable to make plans, go out, or take calls. It was all rather mysterious at first and then simply faded into "I can't because it's when my sacred Balinese women's group meets." There would be a new deity or statue on her altar at her house and when asked about it, of course, it too came from an elder in this secret group.

All of this was well and good, and the girl was in no way jealous of Dilly. In fact, since Dilly's stupid husband had cheated on her and she had filed for divorce from his ugly ass . . . this was the happiest she had seen her in a while. The girl was really happy that Dilly had found a new sense of belonging—a healthy one that seemed to bring her great pleasure.

One night, Dilly called to ask if she would like to attend a very special invitation-only secret sacred sisters meeting, and the girl said why not? It seemed to bring Dilly a lot of joy and she could use some of that these days. So, she said yes, and the wheels of sacred sister fortunes were put into manifest-motion.

These women met weekly over Zoom, so obviously the technology in Bali was strong. The girl was a little nervous and excited to learn more about these special women. She took her time getting ready before the meeting began; she did a full face of makeup, washed her hair, and wore her favorite shirt and jewelry for the call. After all, what does one wear on a super-secret sacred Balinese women's group call? She thought it was important that she try to look her best and was sure Dilly would do the same for her.

Once on the call, it was a little like being trapped in the Brady Bunch Squares, but with incense. All the faces of the members were squished into tiny technicolor square boxes. The algorithms matched your screen with whomever it felt like and you couldn't see yourself when it was your turn to talk; rather, you would be facing tiny women you had never met before in your entire life. Estonia, Bali, Texas, Dubai, Marrakesh, and California were all joined into one on the screen.

"Welcome sisters, tonight we have a very special guest joining us. Let us pass the magic wand to her after our meditation please. Join sister Mary, as she leads us now. I want all of you to close your eyes as we gather together in a field far, far away. We are surrounding an elephant oak tree that is centuries old. Tiny fireflies sing and dance around it with us in the evening mist as we make our way into a circle of movement and motion, dancing around and around her thick trunk," sang the heavily accented voice of the elder.

The girl kept her eyes closed and tried to enjoy the corny opening meditation. She kept an open heart and an open mind and waited for the next set of instructions to come.

"Tonight's topic is remembrance. Remember a time when you felt totally supported by the Universe. Remember, what are the colors and images around you? Let this guide you to consider what areas of your life need support and healing from the universe now."

One by one, the faces of each of the sisters in the colorful boxes blew up to fill the screen, as they each spoke on the topic for five full minutes. There were many answers—one lady said, "Peace," while another said, "Debt-free and in touch with my body" and another "Breathe." It didn't at all make sense to the girl, and before it was her turn to talk and introduce herself to the group, the leader came on to remind them all to write a letter to their Divine this week. Shit, there was homework? Great.

They spoke a lot about being among the chosen tribe, among my chosen family, in the conscious crew, but it sounded a little forced to the girl.

And just when the girl thought she might bounce; a leader took the wand and spoke words that rang true in the girl's heart:

"A life of meditation with the sisters is about recognizing the patterns in our life.

Our grandmother oak.

The sentinel, who weathers and listens.

An elder who learns from us over the ages.

As tribes create families . . .

Why does growth have to be painful at first?

Why is laughter so close to pain?

Working with one's self, accepting oneself, recognizing that out of one's pain comes resilience.

From being broken comes gratitude.

Depth and beauty are born of authenticity.

To be able to have and to hold compassion for humanity is to step into our power.

And how in the beginning and in the end, I came here to find myself."

And those were the magical words she needed to hear, the ones that pulled her in.

The masterclass introduction call went so well that the triad of leadership, or the "Mama Llamas" as they liked to be called, invited her to attend a one-on-one with just the three of them and Dilly. It was during this special meeting that they asked the girl if she would like to join their holy group. She was told she could seek comfort in the secret sacred all-women's Balinese group in a tribal three-part ceremony, for the sacred non-refundable contribution of only $5,000.00 USD.

These women met weekly over Zoom. So, obviously, these sacred sisters' psychic signals were not strong enough to transcend the miles, and thus, they succumbed to the use of technology to facilitate oneness. It felt nice to meditate with them weekly and journey out to guided fields and dance around mystic trees with fairies, by streams and under rainbows.

The Mama Llamas would take turns opening the meetings and leading the ladies through guided meditations. Some would chant or sing soft lullabies in Sanskrit or play the harmonium as they led the ladies further and further away from the troubles and worries of their daily lives, entrancing them with their spell-like words, emphasizing slow deep breathing until they were almost on the verge of falling asleep. Then, boom!

They would "put down the magic wand" and open the floor so that any sis-star who felt moved to share could pick it up and begin speaking. Each week a new topic was pre-selected. The ladies would get it sent to their "spiritual e-mail," and they were to meditate on the theme until it was their time to speak.

Sometimes, the prompt was like "Remember a time when you felt completely loved and supported by someone." Other times, something like "Imagine you could have one power in your life right now. What would it be and how would you use it?" It was a little cheesy, yes, but the harmonium and the music made it seem a little more magical than it really was. And then there were those rare golden moments when a woman's voice would speak clearly and drop serious wisdom among the sis-stars. They didn't wear costumes or glitter gel; nobody wore Mumu or got high. They were just a group of normal, everyday women with normal routines who were looking for a little bit of magic in their lives.

As members of this super-secret sisterhood, they each pledged to show up for weekly meetings prepared and ready to participate and contribute. Once in a while they would take turns sharing the opening meditation or chanting the closing mantra. The emphasis of these meetings was peace and love. That was it. Until the day the girl came to the group needing to vent about the sexual trauma she had just lived through. That shifted everything.

She had fulfilled her commitment to the group, always bringing her turbo-love-light-and-joy to every meeting. Often, as a writer, her prepared notes and topics inspired the others in terms of clarity, humor, and feels. The stories she brought were consistently happy, bright, inspired anecdotes carefully crafted to uplift the sisterhood and leave them feeling recharged. She enjoyed playing this part for them and found some pleasure and comfort in her role. That is, until the night she needed them, and they ultimately weren't present for her when she needed them most.

It was the night her boss had tried to lure her to his hotel room down in San Diego, a second time. He had just flown back into the states from Heathrow and had requested her presence for a meeting. He asked her to make reservations for dinner at nine, but most kitchens were closed on a Monday night that late, leaving the only possible alternative: his hotel restaurant. He texted her his room number as she was driving down, presumably for valet parking, but also, on account of him being a major douche, because he fully intended to try to get her into his room.

Upon her arrival at the hotel, she valet parked her car and texted her boss that she had a meeting for an hour and would call him after. She searched the lobby for a quiet place to join her meeting but couldn't find one. She settled for the disabled stall in a remote women's bathroom. She placed her briefcase over the toilet, creating a seat, put her ear buds in, and joined the call.

The call opened with a five-minute meditation in silence. Then the night's topic was announced, and the "magic wand" was opened to the floor and whoever felt like sharing first would start in. She usually hung back, but tonight; she was the first one on.

"Hey guys. I have something to share tonight that is really important. I've been holding something inside me now for weeks and I have to let it out. This is really hard to say so here goes—three weeks ago, I was raped by my boss and his friends at a work event." The tears flowed. Her voice stopped and cracked as she choked on her emotions all coming out of her now at once. She had been holding it inside of her and it felt so good to speak her truth in a safe place.

She stared back into the tiny technicolor Zoom faces of her sisters on the screen, looking like the Brady Bunch squares, as many of the sisters around the world on the call stared back at her, crying in silence.

"I'm here, calling you all from a bathroom stall in a hotel in San Diego right now, and my boss, the one who attacked me, is upstairs waiting for me. You see, he wanted to have another 'meeting' about my 'promotion' and demanded I come here. To be clear, I am not going up to his room as he's requested; instead, I'm going to meet him in the lobby restaurant. I am scared but also feeling strangely empowered. I met with an attorney and the authorities today and filed claims against him.

"I am okay right now, or, well, I will be. As you can imagine, it's been incredibly hard to function," she said as she wiped her nose on the corner of her good winter coat.

"I am going to make it through this. I am not going to let this vicious act define me," she said, more for herself than for them. "I love you sis-stars. Thank you for holding space for me tonight. I wanted to go first because I have to leave you now and head into this meeting."

No doubt, she had needed the solidarity and safety of her sisters now more than ever, which made what happened next even worse. As she looked into the faces of her sis-stars, she saw many tears reflected back at her. Her pain had been felt and they were sending her love and well wishes. Meanwhile, her asshole boss was texting her and pestering her, trying to get her up to his room. She needed to focus and get him to meet her in a public space, so she reluctantly left the group Zoom call.

The next day she received a call from the highest mother leader figure (who also just happened to work as a talent recruiter in HR for Big Global), asking her to attend a special call with the triad leadership, regarding her recent share. At last, she thought! This was the moment all of the answers of the great sisterhood were going to be revealed to her at 7:00 p.m. EST. They were finally going to share some magic with her that would help heal her and soothe her tired, worried, anxious, and traumatized soul. In the coming days, looking forward to this meeting brought her great comfort, where previously there had been none.

The night of the meeting, she tuned into her Zoom call and saw the faces of not three, but two of the sisters: the elder and her guru/apprentice. They began with a small prayer and then moved into the topic of the special meeting and proceeded to blindside and rip another hole deep into her gut. She was, they said, too dark for the group. Her recent share had violated the sacred pact to only bring joy and love to the sacred circle. Which was TOTAL BULLSHIT because life is not all love and joy and even her best friend who brought her to the fucking sacred stupid $5,000.00 women's group went through regular life caca and cried on her calls and shared real life shit. How could the leadership of this fucking holy wanna-be-shamanic-elevated-my-ass group not have protocol for actual life events? Loved ones die. Lovers leave. Children get sick. Animals are lost. Disease happens. And what then? When people get mugged on the subway then share with a group the day after, is that not allowed? If your dog goes missing, sorry, that's not sacred, so you're out? Please mourn the loss of your loved ones alone and get the fuck out. Really? When she told of her being raped, the sisters decided that the best they could do was suggest she take a mandatory hiatus while she worked on being less dark, alone. And then they would entertain her re-joining the group. *Really?* thought the girl. *Well, FUCK THAT!*

They cast her out of the divine order for sharing the story of her rape and "being too dark." It seemed her sacred sisters could suck it.

She demanded her money back. But that didn't mean a thing. No, they had kicked her when she was down. Imagine—a grown, supposedly "enlightened" group of women, turning their backs on a fellow member when she was gang raped and had come to them for guidance and help. And they turned her away and voted to reimburse her fees. What total and utter bullshit. How sad it made her feel. She felt betrayed, she felt alone, she felt scared and hopeless and abandoned. This was so unfair and cruel. Before this moment, she didn't think there could be a new level of low to feel, but this cast her down to the bottom of the darkest mental and spiritual cavern in complete isolation. Her flame had sputtered and all but extinguished itself on the long dark fall to the end.

They had killed her soul. She turned to Quan Yin, the deity on her corner table, next to the "courage" ceramic they had gifted to her the moment her first installment of $2,500.00 had cleared, picked it up, and hurled it out the window where it broke like her spirit into a thousand fragments onto the empty black street below. Fuck you to the soul group.

CHAPTER SIX

Meat Hell

Living back with her mom and dad at forty-something, she was certain she had hit rock fucking bottom with a sunflower twist.

She loved her dad and mom dearly and was grateful their unconditional love was a safety net. Her sweet suburban parents meant well. When they came to visit her before she had to file for her first ever and only bankruptcy, they had seen the mountain of bills covering her dining room table. They asked all the right questions and heard all the worst possible answers. She truly had no way out of this at the time and, against all reason but mostly for her son, she choked on her pride, sold almost everything, and moved them both back in with her parents.

This was the time of the holy trinity. You see, she didn't know that taking Xanax, Soma and Norco with some wine could shut down your respiratory system for good. The doctors never warned her. In fact, it was only thanks to the feeling like she couldn't breathe as she tried to drift off to sleep at night that she decided to ask Uncle Google about such things. This was when the all-knowing holy trinity was revealed. As Uncle Google told her, "The Holy Trinity" is a drug regimen that includes at least 1 opioid, a benzodiazepine, and carisoprodol. Opioids, benzodiazepines, and carisoprodol all have some overlapping side effects in terms of drowsiness, respiratory depression (opioid), confusion, tremor, and seizures risk.3-5 When combined, these drugs are synergistic in causing respiratory depression and could collectively result in death."

Adding this to the daily day drinking helped her forget the shit hole that her life had become. Wrestling with her shrink and her mind to try to find a place of gratitude for such basic facts (such as being alive) after surviving the recent massive traumas felt impossible. Forget that the wine she could afford was shit and that the vodka tasted of cheap alcohol, she had some very real problems. Between the pills and the booze and the meat diet her mom pushed onto them with her well-intentioned heavy Catholic guilt, she was pretty much fucked or at least felt like it. She knew they meant well, but man, was it hard to remain soft and graceful. She tried to accept their help, but it was hard as it came with every childhood and lifetime trigger, she had been determined to shift.

She wasted away just over a year behind that guest room door. A year of not backing up her computer, a year of not living life. People get sick and have less than that to live, and here she was, trying to finish herself slowly. It wasn't that she was suicidal—it was just that she was so low and so alone while being so low, that it felt like she might as well continue the numbing. So, it was with great sadness that she ushered in the darkness of the night before its time, so she could drink more readily and finally take the pills so she could pass out.

She was sleeping for more than 17 hours every day, and during the hours she couldn't sleep, she would binge-watch Netflix. This was the sum of her life. It had come to this. A heavy mundane existence, courtesy of the vile acts of the men in charge of Big Global and now her former sacred sisters' group, causing her lows to hit new lows. She mostly laid on the old mattress in the small room with no lock and tried to numb herself or sleep the days away. The only thing that would sometimes pull her up and out of bed, beyond taking her son to and from school, was the smell of her mother's cooking. The scent of garlic and onions frying in a pan called to her as she fantasized about mushrooms sizzling with red peppers and spices. But no. Not in this house. This was a kitchen that only embraced the GMO labels she detested. There was no veggie broth, no sweet potatoes, no whole grains or variety involved. No, Mom's was a kitchen of butter, cheese, red meat, gravy, oil and yet more oil.

Her mother meant well but was absolutely a meat pusher. An excellent old-school cook, but every meal revolved around a slab of meat, intent on perpetuating the decline of our global environment. A hunk of pot roast perfectly pan-seared and sliced hitting the plate with heavy whipped mashed potatoes, peas and carrots smothered with a rich, buttery brown gravy. In this house, salad was just a reason to use Bob's Bleu Cheese dressing, garlic croutons, and bacon bits, and, of course, more cheese.

Every day she would remind her mother that she really didn't like to eat meat, and every night her mother would ask how many tacos she wanted or ribs, or rib eye, or chicken breasts, or meatloaf, meatballs, meat, meat and more meat. She was living in a meat hell.

And, of course, everyone knows what sugary wines pair best with meat—dark juicy Cabs or Merlots or heavy Zins. Yes, it was night after night of a heavy wine and meat fest that added not only pounds to her waistline, but heaviness to her heart.

Her heart. The only thing she had to look forward to were her nightly calls with Djedi.

The phone rang and she answered with, "Hello Chérie!" as checked her angle, tilting her head back to hide her double chin.

"Bonsoir, mon amour," he said, his face tired while coming home from work on the metro.

The signal always sucked at this time on his daily commute home; the constant call drops frustrated her to no end.

"Hello? Hello?"

"You can hear me?" Hello?" echoed across the miles.

"Yes, I can hear you!" *Stop saying the same shit,* she wanted to scream. *I've been waiting to hear your voice all day so please say something meaningful,* she thought.

It was their only conversation and the beginning of the end for them.

The girl had no privacy in Casa de Carne. The door to their tiny guest bedroom had no lock, and so her already somewhat limited masturbation sessions came to an end too. Everything went to hell once she was living back in this house. If you could even call it living. Her green tea gave in to coffee and she stopped making her weekly pot of chai. Vegetables succumbed to bread and cheese to compliment the meat regime. Her plants all died as her yoga mat gathered dust, and she felt unremarkable and utterly alone.

She made small efforts to look cute for Djedi on their video calls together, but even those dwindled from what had once been every night to only once a week, eventually stretched further and further out. She wanted to write him a poem or a letter to let him know she still loved him. But did she? She was so disenchanted with where she was and so far away from the happy bright independent woman he had met, she began to self-sabotage their relationship without ever meaning to. She would get increasingly frustrated by their crappy connections and when she finally could hear his beautiful voice clearly, he had nothing to say. Just the same old shit, over and over. She searched her heart for a touch of romance and longed to bring it back. She had begun praying again, as her faith slowly returned, flowing into her empty hours alone.

Once again, life seemed to be showing her through its long winding back alleys toward the paths to redemption, requiring resilience. The gratitude she had once felt with the dawn of each new day staged an ever-so-subtle return in-between her EMDR treatments and her plant medicine ceremonies. She was able to see her patterns more clearly and was eager to get herself the fuck out of this meat house hell and get back with the living.

She abhorred the ungrateful waste her life had become. This was not her.

She had applied to receive unemployment, qualified for the max, and watched her monthly income reduced by over 87% to a pitiful $900.00 every two weeks. She didn't need the added stress of the bill collectors calling and calling and calling her phone daily, so she saved her tax refund and used the money to pay for her chapter 8 bankruptcy, but there was nothing fun about it.

What little activities she used to share with her son and bond over, like taking him out to dinner for poke bowls or frozen yogurt, stopped. As did movie nights or sleepovers at their house with his friends. He was sleeping on a sofa bed in an even smaller room than hers. They each lacked privacy and their relationship suffered too. Although the boy did his best to understand what was happening, there was no denying the psychological impact of a single mother losing what little they had as the boy turned 13. She remembered from her college psych class that children began viewing the world and identifying in socioeconomic terms right around this age. Which sucked, given their present situation. Old, gifted bucket that hurt both their backs, check. Tiny rooms in the house with bad vibes and no privacy, check. Zero money, check. Yup. Times were hard and they needed a miracle.

And while they may have had no things, well, they had each other. They had their health and an awkward temporary roof over their head, but beyond that the tensions ran thick in this old stucco tract home in the middle of the suburbs. She did her best to turn this into a teachable moment for him. For she had always believed in leading by example. That even modeling how to face and survive extreme adversity with grace was important. That being a living embodiment of love and light would count for something. But lord knows it wasn't easy—hell, even her cat hated her for this new and intense negative vibration environment.

It was here, from the rocky bottom of her new reality, that she knew with absolute certainty that her rebound would be a magically epic event. It just had to be.

CHAPTER SEVEN

Nada

Almost two months after her attorney sent over the contingency paperwork for her to sign and return, he sent an email to all of the C-levels, legal team, and HR at Big Global officially outlining the girl's case and claims against them. That night the girl felt she had finally won a small victory and had taken a step forward in her journey to seek justice. Unfortunately, this feeling would end in a matter of hours, when she rose early to take her daily walk—the only healthy part in her daily routine apart from a light and empty alcohol-and-Xanax-induced sleep.

On good days, she would wake up early and go for long soothing walks around and around the same neighborhood loop. Her eyes scanned the land ahead, looking for rattlesnakes, coyotes, and occasionally hawks. On the morning the Ogre sent official letters and legal matters to all of the principals and legal team at Big Global, she was followed.

It was 5:00 a.m. on a cold, cloudy winter morning and still dark out. She shut the front door behind her as she had done a thousand times and dropped her keys behind the plant pot on the porches corner, lured by the false sense of security the suburbs provided. Once out on the road that was her parent's house, she put her earbuds in and began walking toward the golf club to the south. At the top of her street, she turned right and noticed a white Toyota Prius pull out onto the street behind her. It became painfully obvious that it was following her, trailing right behind her at two miles an hour. Its windows were tinted, making it hard to see inside and she could barely see the driver. She thought she caught a glimpse of an older white male with greying hair, but she couldn't be sure.

The girl's heart began racing as her mind flooded with panic. She was certain that Big Global had hired a hit man to take her out. She imagined a scope projecting a small red target onto her back. Fueled by this very possible scenario, she sprinted forward up toward the golf course, where she knew the landscape crew would recognize her and help her. She ran as fast as a chubby girl with back surgery done on her L5 five years ago could muster. The Prius followed along the road, accelerating, not letting her out of its sight. It pulled just ahead of her on the dark, foggy road as the engine stalled and made an odd sound, as Priuses often do.

The girl had the sense to dial in the numbers 911 into the keypad on her phone and she frantically pressed the buttons.

"911—what's your emergency?" came the voice of a female operator.

"Help! I'm being followed by a man in a car—a white Toyota Prius. I'm out walking alone, and I need help now!" she wheezed.

"Where are you right now?" asked the officer.

"I'm on Arroyo Vista by the Tijeras Creek Golf Course and I'm running—please send someone quick! I'm running away right now!" said the girl between gasps for air.

"Okay, I am with you. Officers are on their way. I'm staying on the line with you," said the voice.

"Fuck!" she thought, now panicked. She quickly turned and changed direction, running off the road into the dense brush that twisted down into a deep ravine. Her heart was pounding now, her fight or flight instinct activated—she was in full-blown survival mode. She did her best to stay out of sight, but it all happened so fast.

Up ahead was a clear stretch of the ninth hole, all perfectly manicured golf course grass. She knew if she kept running along the edge of this hole, it would practically lead her to the road that leads to the clubhouse. She stayed the course and never looked back. Thoughts of a bullet whizzing into her back as she ran for her life filled her head and fueled her impossible sprint. The air in her lungs burned, but not as much as the pain shooting down her left hip and leg and into her still-nerve-damaged left foot.

After what seemed like a blurry second, she emerged on the path some five minutes later as a hot sweating mess, slowing to a clumsy soccer mom walk at full speed. Arms swinging, her breath failing her, she finally saw the clubhouse up ahead through the thick fog with its warm lights glowing in the cold damp morning. Overwhelmed by a surge of hope, she began to run like hell again for the last stretch.

"Caller are you there?" asked the operator.

"Yeah—I—am—running!! I'm trying to get away from this asshole in the Prius! I can't breathe!!!" said the girl. *FUCK!!!* she thought. *I'm fat, panicking, and asthmatic! Stop making me talk, lady.*

"Where are you now?" asked the operator. "We've got a car pulling around heading toward the main parking lot of the golf club on Antonio. Can you head there? What is your address?"

"I can't," she wheezed. *How the fuck am I supposed to give you my address...* thought the girl *...while I am running for my life and I can't BREATHE!* No sooner did this thought erupt and dissolve than she saw a pro shop employee up ahead.

She ran up onto the concrete, out of breath, and startled the man.

"Help! I need help! Someone's following me!" she spat out, before she turned toward the grass and vomited.

The operator on the line was full of questions, who she was with, where she was now, and so on. She waited for the sheriffs to arrive up at the clubhouse. And she waited and waited. Eventually she hung up the line with the 911 lady. She was insulted by their casual non-appearance and decided the coast was clear to begin walking home. The sun was up now, and the streets were fairly busy with locals driving to work, jogging, walking dogs, and hitting balls. She was fairly certain no one was going to off her in broad daylight on a golf course.

She was overly cautious and tried to walk mostly through bushes and managed to make it back to the house safe and sound. As she reached down for her keys, she silently swore to herself that she would never walk again. No way. Just as she closed the door behind her, a squad car pulled up in front of her house. *Great timing, assholes*, she thought. *Where the fuck are the police when you need them?* 20 minutes and one report later, she was back up in her room where she would likely spend the rest of the day with her cat, her computer, her pills, and the rest of yesterday's bottle of wine.

But at least she was alive. One thing was certain: She felt absolutely positive that this was a scare tactic being orchestrated by the fuckwits at Big Global. It had their scummy signature all over it. As she stood in her mom's kitchen, making toast and her son's lunch, she told them about being followed and chased. Between the retelling, she made two calls. One to her shrink to get some help navigating this new unsafe feeling, and one to her attorney to tell him what had happened less than 12 hours after he sent the email out.

Her shrink sent her a text asking if it was an emergency; it was Rosh Hashanah, and she was back east visiting her family. The girl made a mental note not to get followed by possible hit men on Jewish holidays.

The shrink told her she would be available for an emergency phone call later in the day, and in the meantime called in another prescription of Xanax to her local Walmart pharmacy.

Meanwhile, her attorney replied to her email saying:

"It is clear that they had hired a PI to pry into past life events, to produce and assemble content specifically designed to make you look unflattering. Don't worry about it. We've got the upper hand."

Seriously, she thought. *But I've done nothing wrong.* And that was perhaps the most difficult thing for the girl to wrap her mind around. She was a hardworking, dedicated, loyal, and talented employee. *Nothing* the girl did was illegal or wrong. *They* raped her. *They* fired a disabled person protected under the Family and Medical Leave Act, otherwise known as the Fuck My Life Act. *They* were just trying to cover their asses with a used pre-spittle moistened Alabama wet-wipe and failing miserably as karma insisted. *They* paid a C-level employee to lure her out into public places and sexually harass and abuse her —quid pro quo. *They* were the big evil here. She was clear on this much. And she was clear that *they* would pay *her* for the irreversible heart damage, emotional damage, and life loss damage that they had done. And now they invaded her privacy and terrified her publicly and had likely just taken away her one last healthy ritual, her morning walk. When would it end?

Her life flipped. She was now a closed person and kept most of her life hidden behind her bedroom blinds. She had become a depressed person when pushed into anxiety-triggering positions, like they had just put her into, and it was *not* okay.

Behind her bedroom walls she was miserable and hiding from life. It would take her losing 25 pounds while holding onto her spirit, her essence, and her mind for any of this to make sense. The clock had ticked away over one year—31,556,926 seconds, 525,948 minutes of her life essence just absolutely wasted. Gone.

Poof. Nada. Never to return. And what *would* return would be so different—it would never replace them stealing her time and scarring her for life or the precious gift of time, which cannot be replaced.

In the last three months, she had been gang raped, wrongfully terminated, and was left with no job. She had lost her home, moved back in with her parents at forty-something, had turned to pills and booze, gained weight, had to file for bankruptcy, was chased by a lunatic PI, was unable to see her fiancé, and kicked out of an alleged sacred women's group for being raped. Oh, and Chump was elected new leader of the free world. Yup. She was pretty sure she needed a reboot but needed to hit bottom first.

Instead, she turned headfirst into the bottom of every bottle she could afford. Her days were built around three things: taking her son to school, buying more wine, and picking him up safely before she could hide back up in her tiny room and pour another glass of wine. Everything else did not require being sober; therefore, she could accomplish it from home. She was coping, managing, and dealing the best she could. No, it wasn't her first choice and she wished things were different, but they weren't. She was stuck until this settlement business was behind her. Nothing exciting to say about day drinking, except that it made it easier to take long naps and fall asleep. That was all she was really trying to do: numb the pain, self-medicate, and pass the time. Which was a shame; life is precious and every second she wasted made her shirk.

What, she thought, would she do differently if these were her last moments on Earth? She would swallow more pills and booze and dance barefoot on the grass. Except for the shame she felt being naked, thanks to the extra weight being a sudden alcoholic put on her. That's what it was: She had become addicted to escape. Addicted to numbing and dumbing herself down.

She was on her way downstairs to refill her small empty jam jar with more hooch when a commotion in the corner living room caught her attention. There, on the carpet, was her mother's 85-pound Golden Retriever humping one of the couch cushions *again*. Having a full raging shag, on the go. This fucking dog was always fucking the couch cushions!

"Cooper! Naughty boy! Stop having sexy time with the couch pillow!" she yelled, trying to snatch it back without touching any dog slime at the same time.

"I frigging swear! They ought to teach you better manners, Coop! This is some bullshit! Every freaking day I catch you having sexy time with mom's pillow! Gross! Go in time out! Kennel, NOW!"

It was annoying and had become one of her pet peeves since they'd been here. This beautiful dog ran rampant with no manners. Just a big sweet empty lug. Ugh. Her mom could love a dog and feed a dog and pick up its poop, but was it enough? How satisfying was this dog's life? It had shelter and the basics, but no training. No toys. No activity. So, it resorted to stealing her pillows for sexy time, all the time. Well, she wasn't an expert on canine care, and she had other fish to fry. She released the dog from his time out and headed to the bar to fill her glass, as she silently swore that if she ever got a dog, it would be well-trained and loved.

Learning to coexist with an 85-pound Golden Retriever who liked to hump old couch pillows and had no training whatsoever sucked. Basically, Cooper was an accurate portrayal of the type of parenting she had received, except she never begged for food from the table, jumped on people, or humped pillows.

But what was it really about her mom that annoyed her? There were some deep wounds there she would need to face in order to heal and release them. So, it wasn't the humpy tea-bagging dog. Maybe the dog was a trigger for all the douchey men that exist?

She could spot them from a mile away . . . the penniless cool guy sponging off naive women sleeping in their spaces, doing drugs, all in the name of being a wanna-be-shaman. The corporate asshole with his suits and ties and cars and bills and debts and fears and poor excuses for open misogyny. The fake nice guy who was secretly addicted to porn of all types, including but not limited to your sister, Tinder, Grindr, and all web-based sexual solutions. The daddy type, older, second marriage failed, kids everywhere who only call when they need money or want something, so yeah, when they need money. All of them insulting, all of them underestimating your emotional intelligence, counting on you to be blind to your self-worth and wooed by the promise of whatever it was they ensured they would give you later, if only you would do something for them first. This cycle was more like a cyclone, or at the very least a heavy shit storm. This was the kind of truth that never made it onto a thank you card. Could you imagine? What if a greeting card line was launched, and everyone in the world knew of its existence. Your job as a good human was to send the warning/thank you card to the unsuspecting party. "Didn't see that coming, did you douchebag?" or "For fuck's sake, get over yourself!" or "Congratulations on your new STD!" Boom. Viola! If nothing else panned out, at least she would have a great idea for a greeting card company.

CHAPTER EIGHT
Dilly

The eventual road to recovery began in an unexpected place. Her best friend had fallen in love with an Iranian man who was trimming weed at a grow house in Riverside. She heard all about the success they were having at this magical house, treating lost souls for anxiety, depression, and drug addiction by using sacred traditions featuring plant medicines. Specifically, Sapo and psilocybin. Never in her life had she journeyed with plant medicine, mostly because of the fear locked in her throat chakra.

So, when Dilly asked if she wanted to join her, she felt absolutely scared, but since she trusted Dilly's wild heart, she knew she would be able to help her find her way out. Drastic measures, she thought, and that was that. She was told to bring an all-white outfit to wear for the ceremony and to not take any pills or meds for at least 24 hours before she got there. Like that was going to happen. Yet, surprisingly, deep down the girl must have been serious about getting clean, because she actually managed to not swallow her pain pills and bathed in lavender instead of nibbling tiny blue football-shaped Xanax.

The girl stood out on the curb with her small overnight bag waiting for Dilly to pick her up. She had bought some orchids and wine to take as gifts to the house. Dilly pulled up in her Ford Flex and the girl hopped in.

"Hiya babes! What's up?" the girl asked as she hopped in and swung the car door shut.

"Come here, you! It's so good to see you! What's all this?" Dilly asked.

"Oh, you know, the usual. You don't arrive at someone's home for the first time without gifts, so I bought a few things." She began nervously tapping her fingers against the window button.

"Are you excited?" Dilly asked.

"I'm more nervous than anything, but I'm excited to meet your friends. Can you turn it up?"

As a Massive Attack song filled the car with familiar vibes, the girl thought about what a year it had been. Watching the towns drift by as they made their way off the toll road and onto the long country backroads.

They pulled up to the house at almost midnight and discovered that everyone in the house was still up. The owner of this beautiful house in Riverside (never had the words beautiful and

Riverside gone together until now) was Sima, a beautiful older woman with a killer body and an even better spirit standing in the foyer to greet them.

"Hello there, darling," Sima purred as she pulled the girls into a deep hug.

"You must be Dilly's friend! Do come, come put your things down and come sit with us," she said as she turned, leading them both into one of the most beautiful spaces she had ever seen. The couches and big overstuffed chairs were all white with large pillows and silk Persian rugs covering the light grey hardwood floors.

She looked around the room and was introduced to some very good-looking people. There was Dimo and his brother Navid, the ceremonial priest. Then there were Shahab, Afshar, and Naiel, three very handsome men. Dilly, a girl named Lolly, Yesinia, Sima, her assistant Mama Joon, and the girl completed the group.

They all sank into the comfort of the living room with its high arched ceilings above and a large brick mantle fireplace that extended into two rooms, as Sima led the conversations. It was the smoothest intake process she had ever encountered.

"Tell me love, what brings you here?"

"Well, Dilly is my best friend and told me about her amazing experience in the ceremony with you all here. She said you are an incredible healer, woman, and guide, and I trust Dilly, so I took a leap of faith and here I am."

"What else?"

The girl looked around the room and hesitated. The last thing she wanted to do was vomit her personal truths here in front of these elegant strangers. But as she looked around the room, she saw—or, rather, felt—love. Which is why even she was surprised as she said . . .

"I've been depressed lately and very unhappy. I recently suffered a very violent trauma and I am having a really hard time healing. I haven't been happy in my skin for months."

"What are you using? Are you taking any drugs or medicines? Do you drink alcohol?"

"Yes, and yes. I've been taking alprazolam for over ten years, more now than ever before, and I take Vicodin sometimes for my back and neck and nerve pains and carisoprodol for relaxing tension. And yes, I drink red wine daily. Also, I've been smoking cigarettes which is an old pattern of mine that I hate. And that's it."

"And when is the last time you took any of this?" Sima asked, nodding her head up and down in an understanding gesture with her hands folded as a temple underneath her chin.

"Yesterday morning I took one Xanax. That was the last time."

"Good. Then you will do the ceremony with us." Sima turned to her apprentice and spoke rapidly to her in Farsi. "I asked her to prepare the tea for our guests." She said, standing.

The girl was nervous about drinking the tea—what was in it? Was the ceremony beginning already? She was struggling to contain her apprehension and felt bad about questioning this nice woman's harmless offer to tea, but she had never been in a shaman's weed house on the eve of a psilocybin journey, so to be fair, she had her room for doubts.

"Here, come, let's sit outside while Mama Joon makes the tea!" Sima announced as she rose, clapping her hands three times in the air, and they all rose and silently followed her outside into the backyard.

Walking out into the backyard was like walking into a midsummer night's dream. There was a small pond, with picture perfect landscaping and white string lights hung all around the pond, illuminating the beautiful flowers and benches, and seating areas all around. All that was missing was a white swan floating in the middle of the pond.

There, attached to the back of the house, were two trundle beds that had been built into the side of the home, so that someone could sit or lie down on them as they looked up into the starry night sky, below the full moon and the tall eucalyptus tree's long branches. The air smelled of pine, eucalyptus, and something else the girl couldn't place. It felt safe here in the magical space. Mama Joon came out of the main house carrying a large tray with a beautiful antique tea pot and six tiny glass cups, along with a tray of fresh summer fruits, some toasted bread with butter, and a small jar of sweet carrot jam.

Sima called for them all to come sit and join her on the day beds, and they gathered around.

"Everybody come take some tea now and help yourselves," she encouraged.

"Thank you," said the girl as she waited her turn to fill her cup.

"It is so beautiful here!" she said with stars in her eyes and a smile lighting up her face.

"Thank you! I am glad you like it," said Sima, as she smiled warmly at the girl.

"Look at what the boys here built for me," she said, sweeping her arms wide to indicate the whole backyard area.

Dimo leaned back in his chair, balancing on its back two legs, and smiled at the girl.

As they drank their tea, the girl slowly relaxed and joined in the spirit of celebration, quickly realizing this space was truly magical indeed. Any preconceived notions and fears she had about the upcoming ceremony began to slide away. Her skepticism of what was in the tea she was drinking faded as the mildly honeyed tea soothed her from within.

Sima's hospitality was generous. She could feel it as they continued their conversation and got to know one another as they all settled in. Dimo sat on a small chair next to a table and was rolling a joint.

"Do you ever smoke?" Sima asked her.

"Sometimes, yes," she said, reaching for a slice of watermelon.

"Would you like to now?" she offered.

"No thank you, I'm alright," said the girl.

"Good. Then let's all finish and go get some sleep before the morning." Her eyes met the girl's and she felt safe. It was then that she knew she would follow this woman's guidance and join in tomorrow's ceremony.

They finished their tea and went back into the house to try to rest. The girl lay on one of the long white couches in the front room, unable to sleep. Her mind raced with fear and familiar doubts, troubling her as she stared up onto the high ceilings watching the night's summer shadows play and dance above her. Her throat felt strange and she wondered just what was in that tea she drank. She didn't feel good and thought about reaching into her purse to find just a half a Xanax to help her sleep, but decided against it, as she didn't want it to interact with psilocybin in the morning.

She reached for her phone and checked the time. It was 3:33 a.m. *Well, shit*, she thought. *I might as well go to the bathroom and get ready for the ceremony at 4:00.* She got up and tiptoed to the bathroom in the front hall, where she quickly peed, brushed her teeth, pulled her hair into a messy bun on top of her head, washed her face, and put on some moisturizer. When she walked back out into the front room, Navid and Sima were already up, dressed in all white, busy preparing the circle in the front room for the ritual that was about to begin.

Candles were lit, large square pillows were pulled into a large circle on the floor, rugs and blankets were arranged all cozily as the guests were all waking up, they pulled on their white clothes and took seats next to each other in a circle on the floor. Soft ancient flute music danced to the flicker of the candlelight as Navid sat in the center with an alter before him. With a mortar and pestle, he ground a reddish-brown substance and packed it into veggie caps. As he prayed over his tools and the mushrooms, his mouth moved in prayer as he concentrated on the task before him.

The girl leaned over toward Dilly on her left, stretching her long legs as she did so, and whispered to her, "Dilly! I'm scared!"

"Trust Navid," Dilly said.

And that was that. The girl trusted Dilly and, in that moment, she knew she was going through with this, despite her monkey mind loaded with fear.

Navid began chanting as he leaned in and pushed a small golden bowl before each person in the circle. In the bowl were the exact number of pills he had been guided in his vision to administer to each person. When the bowl came to the girl, there were six pills inside it. The girl looked up at Navid with terrified eyes and was met with a calm and patient smile on his face as he gently nodded his head up and down, letting her know that it was okay and that he would be watching over her.

There was no going back. She took her dose out of the bowl and passed it, now empty, back to the high priest. A glass of water was placed before her and she began swallowing the capsules one at a time thinking...*Oh shit. What am I doing!* Too late—she was all in. Once she surrendered to this, she felt a calm come over her and she began to focus and meditate on holding the good space in her heart and in her mind. She silently sent Dilly love and intuitively knew the others were sending love into her. The room was quiet now, except for the ancient instrumental music still softly serenading them as the candles danced in the circle. She squinted her eyes and peeked around the room once or twice, but all the other eyes were closed. When they had all taken their dose, they were invited to think of their intention, close their eyes, and get comfortable. It was still dark outside, and for the next 45 minutes they held space together, barely moving, with each person having gone deep within to journey.

When she opened her eyes and looked around the circle, she found Navid's gaze directly upon her, smiling gently, making her feel supported; she returned his smile, letting him quietly know she was okay. Her first thought was that she needed to move her body. She looked up at the first rays of light coming in through the big windows to her left. Everything shimmered and sparkled. This first ray of light was as pure as she had ever seen. She rose from her seated position and stood slowly and quietly doing her chubby girl tripping best not to disturb anyone else as she walked toward a small door that led out to the front gardens. The door opened easily as she breathed in the sweet morning air. The plants all seemed animate as they greeted her in secret plant language, which she now understood. The trees breathed in multiple shades of green, hues exploding with breath, as if this was possible. In fact, deep down, she knew this was their ultimate reality; rather, it was hers that was slanted.

Butterflies flew by and a green Japanese beetle flew directly to her, landing on her outstretched hand. It tickled as it landed on her, making her smile out loud. She turned at the sound of the door and looked up in time to see one of the boys in the ceremony walk outside with her. They exchanged big smiles and he walked right over to her and they hugged. Later, she would not be able to remember what she said, but they both laughed deeply before he went on his way, climbing down into the canyon below, basking in the hot sun on a rock much like a lizard, she thought.

She clearly remembered what happened next. As she walked back into the ceremonial room, she saw Sima though the tiny door, a vision of radiant beauty and light. She looked, it seemed, deep into the girl's soul, and opened her arms into a welcoming embrace and held the girl as she melted into her bosom and her soul began to cry. Visions of Earth and animals all washed within her, and it felt her very lungs were part of the Earth; with every breath, with every heartbeat, she became one with all of the nature that surrounded her. The girl stood there for who knows how long, weeping and sobbing and crying and sobbing in the woman's arms, until there was no more time. As time faded, she became aware of this beautiful woman's soft skin—that they stood in the middle of the ceremony room, still surrounded by the others. The eyes that met hers sent love and others rose to come to hug her next. A small seed of comfort could be felt within the girl where before there was none.

The group spent the next five hours exploring, resting, crying, laughing, and playing outdoors together as if they were children. The girl's breaths kept getting backed up in her lungs at first, which she imagined were part of a thick brown, spongy, dense forest. Every time her body tried to inhale, her mind would use fear to block what was natural and right. The breath of life slowly won over her and the priest appeared next to her. "Be calm, my child, I am here. You are okay now. It is safe to surrender. You can breathe," he said, reaching for a small brown glass bottle from within his robe.

She looked up at the priest and said, "See? I'm turning into a fucking mushroom!"

He looked down, gently smiling at her lying still on the couch, as colors danced like sun-kissed liquid stain glass, swirling with glitter as her eyes tried to focus on his face. His long white robes swung next to her face as he poured rose oil on his hands and began to lightly massage her face and forehead.

The oils smelled good and his caring touch calmed her. She looked around the room and saw Dilly crying next to Dimo, and beyond them, saw Sima performing what seemed to be an exorcism on a girl named Lolly. It looked as if she was pushing a long sharp needle into her belly button and cork-screwing out the bad within her. Later, she would share that she had survived sexual assault as a young girl, and that this intuitive shaman was pulling it out, casting out the trauma from her adult body. The girl arched and moaned and writhed on the floor, finally falling into a peaceful trance, having been re-birthed.

The men began stretching their muscles and headed outdoors, some to the pond out back and others to explore the flat rocks on the land further below.

There were three adult ducks near the pond, named Barack, Bush and Trump.

More and more of the girls ventured outside into the sun. Every green tree seemed alive, their colors tripled in rich dimensions, and every living creature became a friend. Each soft breeze against the girl's shoulder brought with its new meaning and insight, as her mind would quickly assign as either funny or triggering an old painful memory. Each moment brought another new opportunity with it.

Sima appeared next to her, staring at the pond, watching two red and blue dragonflies dance around the plant stand poles. She placed her hand softly on the small of the girl's back and the girl raised her eyes to meet Sima's. Within less than a second, the girl began to cry—releasing great moans into the air, startling all the creatures near and far. She was led over to the trundles attached to the back of the house and lay down upon them. Part of her feared that an exorcism like she had seen earlier would now happen to her. And, in part, she was right.

Sima and her assistant gave the girl guided directions, telling her when and how to breathe. The cycle of her breath became hot and fast, then deep and slow. This cycle repeated, in the hot Riverside summer heat, again and again. The girl was completely uninhibited, despite being among these virtual strangers. One boy, it seemed, was looking over at her, standing just out of sight, but remained a force that she could constantly feel. As if he was with her, guarding over her.

Sima barked at the girl, telling her to let it out. Tempting the wounded fragments of the sexual ghosts locked deep within her to come out and play. Once free, they would be cast out of this realm and the girl's body, never to return. The girl raised her head and neck up off the edge of the trundle and let out a scream so loud, surely the others would think she was dying. And in a way, she was.

She could see two giant eucalyptus trees filling the sky over her, providing precious and much needed shade. As she moaned and writhed, and screamed and cried, her strange sounds filling the sky, shattering the hot silent summer day. They raised her slowly—the two women walked her over to a small chair over by the dirty grass. They had dug a hole in the dirt under her chair. Again, she was given instructions and told what to do.

She filled the hole with her doubt. In went the bloodied underwear that she had taken off and shoved into the bathroom trash can on the night of the rape. In went the eyes upon her, their tiny brown bodies above her, and the memory of running half-naked down the hall of the Renaissance hotel corridor, when she had come to. In went all of the zeros in her life, one by one, stacked up there since the night they attacked her. She put her boss's face into the hole, his tiny nubby three-year-old prick into the hole. She put his British accent and phony smile into the hole. She put all the creepy eyeball rape-like leers the men of Big Global followed her with down into the hole. All her pain poured into the hole, until at last she could scream no more.

They put their arms underneath her armpits and carried her up and led her back into the house. The assistant washed her entire body, reaching high under her loose white skirt, rinsing away whatever was left of her shame off of her. As the cool waters touched her hot kappa skin, another torturous memory faded. Sima stood above, swinging an ancient lantern with incense burning within it. The strong smoky odor quickly filled the room. There was a cage on the floor, with two baby bunnies inside. The girl lay down onto the soft silken rug and finally closed her eyes.

It was over. She didn't ever want to open her eyes, for fear that the wretched fearsome memories would return. This rare peace she felt now enveloped her, and it was everything. When she finally did blink open her eyes, the sun had moved, and the room was cool and empty. Sima and her assistant were gone and it was just her and the bunnies. She turned onto her side and lay there watching them for a while. She finally pushed herself up off the floor, and back onto her feet.

Sima walked over to her with a cool glass of water. It tasted of melons and mint as the girl drank it into her very soul. She never wanted this to end. The woman placed a light shawl around the girl's shoulders and gave her a long, long hug.

It was only 8:30 in the morning. The sun rose, bringing with it extreme heat, but they didn't care. Nothing could diminish this natural, peaceful high they were riding. Energy exploded in their cells, coursing through their veins. The girl felt better than she had in many years. She didn't want a cigarette or a drink here. In fact, she only wanted more delicious melon water and lots of it.

In the late afternoon, they were all called in to clean up for the meal. The meal was vegetarian and delicious. Mama Joon and Sima had been in the kitchen together for hours making a big pot of soup, curry, some rice, and bread with butter and jam. A long, large plastic mat was set over the Persian rug in the front room where they had met last night. The girl had never seen such a layout, nor had she eaten a feast from the floor before. I guess, she supposed, this was a weekend of firsts.

Over the next few months, the girl would return to this house for many more ceremonies with Sima and Navid. She would be reborn and bury some old patterns and past life traumas that had been following her into this realm. Together, over the summer of 2018, they would use their magical ceremonies to help the girl wean herself off of the meds and low vibration habits that threatened to kill her.

When she returned to her parents' house, some incredible shifts started to happen. First, she was determined not to eat meat and was fucking serious about it. Second, she intended to switch from red wine to sparkling water from time to time. But the real shocker was the pills. She didn't feel the need to take any of her pills! That in and of itself was a miracle. She had suffered through the worst of her trauma and pain, while maintaining an eternal optimistic attitude. She was finally able to look at all of the choices she had made, dig deep, and was ready to do the work and get on with it. All of these changes within her were pushing the girl to protect and build her immune system. She was sure of it.

The healers encouraged her to go to an RV park called the dunes in the Back Bay of Newport Beach, for micro maintenance ceremonies. It was here that she arrived early one morning, having fasted since the night before. Again, no pills were taken prior.

It was a bright summer morning when she arrived, but typical of the Southern California June gloom, the air still hung all around them like a thick grey veil.

"Come, sit babba," barked Dimo.

"Drink," he said, handing her a large glass bottle of water.

She drank communal water with the Iranian shaman and Dilly outside the tiny trailer, then climbed into a small tent out back.

She had traveled far and had resisted the call of the Kambo, lest her research and fears demanded it as a logical next step in her healing evolution. Her R1 graduate mind was scared and told her there was no need to tattoo tree frog poison in small trailer park tents administered by wannabe shamans whose non-certification came like unwanted coupons in the mail. To her way of thinking, three passport stamps in and out of the Amazon got you some credibility but wasn't entirely without risks. Ping-pong, zing-zing, ding-dong, and you're out.

But her higher divine feminine knew otherwise. So, she entered the tent with Dilly just as the sun was breaking through the fog. Inside, similar to the ceremonial circle at the ranch house, was a round altar built on the floor, set with all the wannabe-shaman's tools. White candles were lit and from the looks of it had been burning all through the night. Curious and scared, she looked at his tools, trying to figure out which among them would burn the small circles into her flesh where the medicine would be placed. She was terrified of watching someone willingly burn a small hole into her body, and all the more so by knowing this was being done specifically to carry the powerful poison through her but shifting was more important than getting caught up in the means to her way out of hell.

Upon tuning into everything he was doing to Dilly, she was immediately filled with dread. She watched as he would hold the flame to a small round object, letting it get hot like a branding iron, then set it aside as he cleaned a spot on the inside of her ankle. Dilly was brave and had many of these small round burns tattooed into both her arms and legs. The girl held her breath as he turned back to the fire and the iron, then prayed for Dilly as he gently pressed it into her flesh. Dilly jumped just a little and he held it to her. She could hear the skin sizzling as he ripped it off and set it aside, reaching for a small vial and a knife. He began scraping a small amount of a gooey poultice onto her fresh wound, and moments later she reached forward for the puke bucket and hurled.

Purging, they called it. And it was just what the girl feared most. Having her breathing somehow restricted or compromised while under the influence. She was entranced by Dilly's experience, knowing she was next. One moment her eyes were fixed on the wannabe-shaman in front of her, the before view, while he blew the tobacco smoke onto his clavicle indent from the Rapa-like pipe and repeated this upon her upper middle back. This was her last vision, as she thought to herself, *The smell of tobacco is strong,* followed in a nano-second by her mind sending a signal to her stomach: *I am going to vomit.* Both signals which were ultimately cancelled out by her supreme spirit saying fuck that shit and instead opting to pass out. She fainted. When her eyes opened next some 30 seconds later, they beheld a new view. *I just fell backwards onto my ass* she thought, as shit got real. She was now being covered in rose water and frankincense oil after being gently moved to a new position, onto her back with both legs extended in the air to rush blood back to her head. The same head which was filled with the perpetual sounds of the summer's green June scarab beetles (which flew right into September) filling her ears and brain at what felt like unfathomable decibels. "Look!" they said as the wannabe-shaman pointed upwards to the tent above her head. "Yes," said the wannabe-shaman, confirming that indeed, one had just flown to the precise spot above her. "No!" she tried to explain but gave up any attempt to use her words. *They are in my head and ears,* she thought. It was clear the wannabe-shaman did not understand her. Alas. Alas was a funny way of saying and meaning "Whatever"—a minor digression suppression mandatory to our psyches' survival in these vibey-vibey times. Alas, she was sure that the wannabe-shaman was not all that.

Yet, the ceremony worked. Despite fainting for the first time in her life, she was alive. It was as if the medicine knew just where to go in her body to heal her. Once the medicine was coursing through her veins, buzzing and rushing blood up into her brain, it made her flush and feel hot. Arms, hands, and feet were tingling with the fire of being lit from within. The frog medicine went deeper still, into her spine where it began to repair her stenosis and bulging discs. There she could feel it linger and burn. Post-ceremony, she couldn't drive for many hours, so she walked down to the sand with a towel and some water and sat in the stillness of the sunshine. Finally, she moved into the water and let the cool wet waters remind her new burns that they existed. She spent many days integrating this experience and saw its effects bleed into her life in many small ways. Sure, she would not ever want to do another maintenance ceremony with the Kambo, but she was grateful for the experience. She had changed her position and thought perhaps Dimo was a magical being after all.

The ceremony had mellowed her out. Before Sapo, Kambo—whatever you called it—she was activated from the psilocybin ceremony but willing to follow the high priest's encouragement to follow up with Sapo.

At times there was still a part of her that wanted to scream. The screams had been stuck inside her for so long, it didn't make sense that they had not escaped or strangled her by now. God, she was so tense, she was ready to pepper spray a ghost. Every sound the wind made spooked her. Tensions under her skin ran as high and overburdened as India's telephone wires.

At least she had the tools and knew now what to do when she felt bad; but she also knew that she couldn't always rely on plant medicine in a pinch. So, she turned inward, to meditation. She meditated from where she was with one of the hundreds of apps on her phone, seldom used. When the annoying guide's voice got to the forgiveness part, she almost choked on her saliva. Never, ever had the girl not sat bolt upright at a meditation's end and said, "Fuck this shit."

Her shaman (her elder) laughed upon hearing this and suggested perhaps she should be living with the "Fuck this shit" meditation for now. And so, it was, lost in an attempt to lose her judgement, she reread the words "There is no right, no wrong." No this, no that. No, no, no. Bonk on the head to the powerful girl. Zing to the heart for the wise woman. Loo loo loo loo loo loo to the inner warrior. And yes, "FUCK THIS SHIT," for now. She was angry and would have to sit in her anger for a while to realize her name was grief. Keeping such great pain close to her heart—carrying the burden and bitch of anxiety and fear for so long—had almost taken all her light. Almost. On the morning her son licked the frog in the mountains and caught the fever, the picture book she made for him arrived. In it carried all the wisdom she could tolerate. Despite the tin men raping her and sucking her life vitals in ways that could not be replenished, she was able to see, in some small ways, that it had not been a total loss. It took real skills to choke on air, fall up the stairs, and trip over nothing. The battle was hers but would require the gifts of others, and the picture book would be key. It was always helpful to have images around her to focus on as she memorized spirit hacks and worked her ancestral magic. This worked to a point too, but after all she had been through, sometimes she needed more.

Truth be told, she carried bear spray—not pepper spray. It came with a warning that encouraged users to read the "how to deploy" manuals before carrying it. It was military grade, whatever that meant. The first sentence described what the defense spray did:

"Bear spray WILL cause: involuntary eye closure, difficulty breathing, facial burning, and psychological symptoms (fear, anxiety and panic)." Say what? She felt as if she had cracked a conspiracy, and that the US Government had been spraying this on all residents since the '70s. This bear spray combined with the non-whole-grain, non-organic-veggie-and-fruit-rich diet, in favor of the fatty, meat-centric, fried, plastic, and preservative filled junk Americans ate, was one hundred percent problematic. Indeed, mixed with the chemtrails? The leftover WWII nerve gas now dropped onto crops that were being fertilized with government leftover toxins. It was no coincidence that people had more anxiety than ever. It seemed to her from her recent experience with anxiety and diet that disease was a choice. One that could largely be healed with consuming clean food as medicine. All these people were consuming dense, fatty, processed shitty foods and had all been bear sprayed as they drank from tainted water supplies filled with antibiotics and pus. No wonder everyone in China walks around with masks over their faces. They didn't want to be sprayed and or they were smart enough post-SARS to value best health practices.

She did her best to share all of her amassed knowledge on nutrition and diet with her bright son. In the mix of her trauma, she was very much aware that her son was also living his own version of this trauma, living in the backlash of the #Metoo movement just like she was. Here was the son of a woman who had been objectified. Another innocent child made to needlessly suffer. It warranted being said that ultimately, these men were hurting the men, too! Talk about idiocy!

Granted, his thoughts and feelings were muted and estranged (thank God), but important, nonetheless. He was embarrassed and followed her lead, not wanting to go outside and play with other kids in the neighborhood. He did not have a space that was really his, and certainly not one he was proud of. It was not a space he wanted to identify with so there were no sleepovers, and the invitations for playdates eventually stopped coming all together. Without their weekend movie dates or fun special sushi dinners, weekends became divided, each of them retreating behind the borrowed bedroom doors of her parents' house.

He was affected by what had been done to her, as it had really been done to both of them. People weren't stopping to think about what the viewpoint of the littles looked like or to consider how parents have to help heal what was broken inside them along the way.

It was thoughts like these that prompted her to have a very open and candid conversation with her son about what had happened to her and to them. She chose a Saturday morning and drove them down to their favorite beach, Treasures Cove down in Laguna. As she drove around the familiar streets looking for parking, she searched for the right words. She surprised herself by offering a silent prayer, and trusted that the right words would find her.

They parked and walked down, taking in the beautiful, lush flowers and deep green plants lining their pathway to the beautiful shimmering blue ocean below.

"Hey buddy. Check in one, two, three," she said.

"Yeah Mom, I'm here," came his little voice.

"Look Mom! Did you see that? That was the California state fish! That orange one right there. It's called a Garibaldi!" he said, with more life than earlier.

"Wow! I did see it! That is so cool, how did you know that?" she asked him.

"From fishing. I'm an ocean fisherman, just like my Dad and my great grandpa Lou," he said.

"Yes, you are. You know, Vinyl, I've been fishing for a way to talk with you about why we moved in with Bubba and Nana this year, and what our plans for the future look like. I thought you might like to help me. First, I am so sorry if any of this has been uncomfortable for you, and I know Mommy wasn't feeling good for a long time, but I'd like to talk with you about it now, if that's okay with you," she said, watching him closely.

"Uh-huh," he said, nodding his head and staring off into the surf.

"Well, you know hon, there were some very powerful men at Big Global, who were very, very evil and they did some very hurtful and damaging things to me, and unfortunately, these things affected not just me, but you are too. I wanted you to know that I understand what you're going through and I'd really like us to get ready to turn the page on a new chapter together and start looking forward together. I know it has been hard for you too and I am so very sorry. I wish I could take it all away . . . but the truth is, it happened, and I can't. But we can focus on moving forward together as one. Would you like to talk about what you would like to do when this is all over?" she encouraged him.

Silence. So, she tried again.

"These bad men are going to have to pay Mommy for what they did. I know it is hard to imagine us having so much one day, when we seem to have so little, but I want you to focus on all that we do have. We have clean water, shelter, and our health and our family and food. Really, we have so much," she said solemnly.

"I hate Nana's cooking, Mom, and her energy is bad."

The girl laughed out loud and told him, "Me too, honey, me too. But like it or not, they were there for us when we needed them and the least, we can do is be respectful toward her. She tries and is really just a young unhealthy purple-blue soul who hasn't evolved," she said, although this was excruciating to admit.

She wasn't sure this was entirely true, and she could never figure out her mom for the life of her. But she didn't want them to get too far-off topic.

"Listen, why don't we think about where we would like to go for a holiday when this is all over? Where would you want us to go? Hmm?"

"Hawaii!" he said, brightening up. "Let's go to Maui, Mom, and bring Bubba with us!"

"What a wonderful idea, Vinyl, that sounds like just what we need. What else?" she encouraged him.

"I don't know. You mean like . . . adventures? Or what?"

"Anything. Let's dream a little," she said, smiling.

"Umm, can we get a new car, a big one that doesn't hurt our backs when we sit in it?" he asked.

"Absolutely. Top of the list. What else, my love?"

"Can we invite my cousins to come to Hawaii with us too?" he asked, looking up at her. It was the first time he turned away from the ocean and the first real smile she had seen on his face in months.

"You bet. You're so sweet. They would love that. What else?"

"And Djedi. We can invite Djedi to come. I bet he will love Hawaii!"

"Agree. I think you're right. He would love it. What else?"

"Can we get our own house again, with a big room for me and a gaming computer and monitor? Can we please?" he asked, doing a little shuffle on the sand with his feet.

"Would that bring you joy? What have you *always* wanted? Always?"

"A puppy! Mom, can I? Can we get my Golden Retriever puppy for real? Can we please?"

"I think that will be the first thing we do once we've got a place to live, yes," she promised.

They spent the next couple of hours enjoying the beach, playing and swimming and searching the tide pools for signs of life. The tides were rising, and they were getting hungry.

"Mom, can I get a crappy meal on the way home? Please?" he pleaded.

"Hard no, buddy. But we can get something a little healthier. How about some nachos or a fish taco from Pedro's and an Orange Bang? Or a bean burrito and some chips and salsa from the spot?" she encouraged him.

"Fine. Whatever, I'm just really hungry. Thanks Mom," he said, giving her a nod of approval.

She had done her best to make this a teachable moment. She believed not in asking kids what they wanted to be when they grow up, but rather asking them what problems they wanted to solve. This changed the conversation from *who* do I want to work for to *what* do I need to learn to be able to actualize my dreams. She hoped this was working with Vinyl. She hoped and prayed that she was modeling how to navigate challenging situations with grace and ease. She was only blessed with her one miracle child, and she didn't want to fuck him up. She had come so far in these past few weeks, and her spirit was gaining momentum. This felt so, so well deserved.

For now, things seemed to be looking up and she needed to stay in the flow. They had been deprived of sunshine for so long, it was time to break out of old patterns that no longer served them. She did the math in her head and calculated how long it would be until her next unemployment check came in. She promised herself she would take the boy out for his beloved poke dinner.

"Hey honey, I really loved today. All your ideas were fantastic. Let's keep thinking about them and we can talk some more when we go out for your favorite poke dinner next week, okay?"

"Thanks, Mom!" he said, lighting up.

They ended their beach day, each with good feelings and hope that tomorrow would be a brighter day for them both. It was the first of many to come, the girl thought as she relaxed her stomach and breathed in from her belly. Deep belly breaths in the flow. For the first time in a long time, she could see her way out of this mess.

In an instant, she had a vision. The shifter was back, crossing dimensions. She was back up in her room at the house, staring out of the window, escaping the blistering heat of the midsummer day when the grid slipped and she saw it, plain as day. Sacred geometric patterns were revealed where normally there was just more sky. The rooftops and the treetops acted as the horizon set point and everything above that slid, revealing other dimensions. As she felt its presence, she felt her negative emotions lifting like a weight off her shoulders. Lifting, lifting, until she was lighter and lighter still. It seemed her angelic golden guides were with her after all. Indeed, she was blessed.

CHAPTER NINE

Ad Astra

An old friend from work reached out to her on LinkedIn and asked her if she wanted to grab coffee or meet up at the farmer's market. The last she had heard; her friend had resigned from Big Global just weeks after they fired the girl. To the girl, it felt like an act of solidarity. Which was why she agreed to meet up with her after such a long disconnect. On the day they met, it was over 101 degrees, so they decided to meet in the mall instead and walk and talk in the AC.

As the girl pulled up to P.F. Chang's, she spotted the lady sitting on a bench in a pink velour jogging suit. It was clear this woman had not done any jogging in a very long time—she had probably gained a hundred pounds since they last met. The girl had recently lost over 30 pounds and was feeling sexy in her cute cut off jean shorts and tiny tank top. She felt bad for the bloated white lady and said so.

"It's so good to see you!" she said as they moved in for a hug.

"Oh! It is so good to see you too! You look great! I mean—amazing! You lost weight and I gained!" she said with a smile, eagerly nodding her head up and down.

"Yeah! Well, um, it is really good to see you too! Shall we walk?"

"Sure, sure. If we walk the perimeter of the shops, square to square, we will get maximum steps in while we visit!" she said as she punched a program into her Fitbit watch.

Why is it that people most out of shape are the most obsessed with fitness apparel and gadgets? thought the girl.

"Um, sure, I mean yeah, okay. I've never strategized how to walk in a mall before," she said with a little laugh.

"Oh, it's a really good way to stay cool and get your steps in. I'm here all the time!" said the lady excitedly.

The girl was sweet and tried to show some excitement, but like a bad date, she knew in the first few moments that this was going nowhere fast. She was already thinking about how to get out of here and they had only just arrived. *Well*, she thought, *I had better make the most of it.*

They walked past the summer store windows and went into Z Gallery. It was one store that wasn't loudly advertising summer bikinis or short shorts or sexy heels, all items that this pink jogging suit lady could not fit into or enjoy.

"So, tell me what you've been up to since I last saw you?" the girl asked.

"Well, since I left Big Global, I haven't gone back to work. The truth is, when I had pieced together what they did to you, I just couldn't stay." The lady ranted about how unappreciated she was at Big Global and whined on and on about what a joke the company was. The girl agreed and said so.

"Yeah, I know what you mean. They are really a bunch of tiny tech dick assholes, aren't they?"

"Yes, they are. What ever happened with your lawsuit?" the lady asked.

"I can't talk about it, or they can charge me back $10,000 per verifiable offense. But we are working toward a settlement. Not enough to replace the lost time off my life and the damage the stress has taken on my heart and relationships. The most precious matters they can never compensate for. But it will be something. More than I've ever had. I'll probably invest most of it after I pay my debts. I'm going to be alright," she said, still trying to convince herself.

"Oh, that's really, really good. I am so happy for you. You didn't deserve what happened to you and watching you go through that and hold your head up high at work every day, well, I really admire your strength. I remember how hard that was on you," said the lady.

The girl remembered sitting in the lady's office, her entire story tumbling out over the desk with a box of tissues next to her. This lady with her now, however disconnected, had been there for her during a very difficult time. She wished that she could help her now and return the favor.

"So, I just lost over 30 pounds using a nutritional cleansing system that is plant based and super amazing. Would you like to try some samples? I'd love to help you if you want . . ."

"Is it like Arbonne?" the lady asked.

"Ummm, what is Arbonne?" the girl said.

"It's an MLM scan that I was involved with years ago. They really stuck it to me, so no. No thank you, if it is an MLM company, then I don't want anything to do with it," she said firmly.

"I'm sorry that was your experience with them—again, I don't know who or what they are, but I do know that I'm a woman just like you who has tried everything for the last 50 years and this really works for my body. Tell me, what does it matter where you buy your products from, Target, Amazon, or my company, so long as it's healthy and it works?" said the girl as she stopped to look into the See's Candies store window.

"Well, I just won't buy from any multi-level marketing-based companies. Would you mind waiting here while I go in for a second? Do you want something?" she asked, eyeballing the sweets in the window.

"No thanks, I'm good," she said, reaching into her purse for her phone.

It was strange, being with this woman. They had very little in common now and she seemed resistant to her attempts to help her. She supposed it was a sign that she needed new friends. So many things in her life were shifting, it seemed only right that her inner environment would change as well. She was waiting for the pink lady to come out of the candy store, when she spotted a picture of a Golden Retriever puppy in a J Crew window and it reminded her of her promise to Vinyl. *One day, baby,* she thought, *one day very soon.*

The lady came out and found the girl, still chewing the sample in her mouth as she said, "Tell me more about the settlement. How is that going? Was my friend able to help you?"

"No. George was really nice, but I ended up going with another firm. Also, um, I can't talk about it. I am doing better now, day by day and all that. And when I'm ready and well, I have a financial advisor who will invest most of it for me. That's really all I can say."

"Uh-huh. What kind of investments are you into?" she said as she opened a butterscotch lolly and stuck it into her hungry mouth.

"Well, I maxed out my Roth IRA, created an S Corp, among other things—but that was before all this mess."

"I only ask because I've been investing for years now and watch the markets closely. In fact, I guess you could say it's what I do now." She bit hard into the pop.

"Yeah, I really don't want to know the daily ins and outs of what's going on. My guy is a really old friend of mine and I trust him completely," the girl said, trying to think of a reason to end their date.

Seeing this woman made the girl feel sad, like when you vomit into your mouth just a little bit? She was special to her because when they fired her, she resigned. She was a witness to her downfall, but now she was just a pain in her ass. It seemed that Big Global had taken so much from her, that no matter how ill-fit the friendship, keeping the lady around proved they couldn't take everything.

The lady launched into a long boring speech about the dangers of investing in the S&P 500 index as the girl checked out. She came up with a reason she needed to go home, and they exchanged emails. The heavy lady who hated MLM and was resistant to using plant-based products to revolutionize her life apparently had no qualms about invading people's privacy, as over the next four months would email insider stock market analysis reports to the girl's primary email, prompting her to block her altogether. Next, thought the girl. Good riddance. Bless and release.

Her phone buzzed with a text alert. It was Dilly. Dilly was off to another of her wild plant ceremonial adventures and needed the girl to watch her tiny house. Eager to playhouse and enjoy some space that was not in her parents' meat-centric house, the girl packed a small bag for her and the boy, went to the market to grab some food supplies, and then headed over to Dilly's.

It was about a hundred degrees inside the trailer as they brought in their groceries and set themselves up in the tiny space. The boy set up his Xbox where the tiny dining table was folded down into a makeshift bed, and the girl threw her small bag and the book she was reading up onto the larger mattress in the loft above. There was a small cat named Ziggy Baba they were to look after. The wild kitten pounced and sprang and mewed and whined, finally settling next to the boy's leg as he zoned out on his game.

The first day was fun. The girl took her book and went down to the beach for most of the long summer day. They made dinner together then sat outside at the picnic table outside. The girl enjoyed her wine and the beauty and freedom of the soft summer evening. It was the only time during the next four days that they didn't come close to killing each other.

How the fuck did Dilly live in 14 feet of space with her gypsy lover, and her two daughters? This was nuts!

"Move your feet now!" she yelled at him.

"I can't see! And I can't move cause there's no fucking room, Mom!" he yelled back at her.

"Don't you say fucking!" she scowled, trying to keep her voice low as all the trailers were lined up next to each other and your neighbors could hear you fart.

"But I learned it from you!" he spat as Ziggy jumped out from under the closet and pounced onto the back of the girl's neck, digging in its tiny sharp claws.

"OW FUCK! Goddamn it! Fucking cat!" she yelled.

"Oh yeah—great one, Mom. See? I told you! You're the worst. I hate you, and I want to go back to Nana and Bubba's house NOW! I hate you!" he said as he aimed his controller at the screen, shooting snipers behind dense trees in the game.

"Don't you say that to me. You have zero appreciation for all I do for you! OW Ziggy Baba! Bad kitty!" she said as she reached her arm behind her neck to feel for blood.

"Here you go again. I'm sick of you saying that Mom. You're so great and perfect and blah, blah. I'm calling Bubba to come pick me up."

"You ungrateful little shit! Do you know what? Fine. Just go. I tried to give us a little vacation here, but no. All you want to do is lie in this hot tin can and play videos all day when all the other kids are outside swimming and living their best life. Great. Just great." She stopped talking as tears welled up in her eyes and her body shook. She didn't know how to reach him lately and it worried her.

She worried about the boy's lack of social skills and activity in general. She was hoping that things would change for the better and that he would appreciate a little escape to the coast for a few days, but no. No matter how many times she asked him to come ride bikes with her, or go swimming, or take a walk to get a soft serve ice cream on the boardwalk, he refused. He had barely brushed his teeth since they got here, and he smelled like she needed to push him into the pool, if only . . .

Her phone buzzed, snapping her out of her thoughts. It was her dad.

"Hello?" she answered.

"What the hell's going on over there?" he barked.

"I don't know, Dad. It's not good," she said, pulling at her full bottom lip.

"You there?" he asked.

She was silent. She knew if she said anything next, she would lose it and cry hard, and she didn't want her son to see her fall apart.

"Hello? Can you hear me? Hello?" he asked.

"I'm here, Dad," she managed.

Then silence. He could hear it in her voice and knew there was trouble. Ever since they had fired her, things had been tense and difficult on everybody.

"Well, you better pull yourself together and bring him home. We can talk then," he said and hung up.

"Son turn that thing off and come here. We need to talk," she said, rising to stand beside him.

"Mom, not now. I just want to go back home."

"I know hon, I know. So, do I. But the truth is that right now we don't have a home. All we have is the kindness of the people who love us most and each other. I can see you're angry with me and at life and it's important to me that I help you. Whatever questions you have, whatever it is that you're feeling inside. Please buddy, let me help you."

The boy looked straight ahead, staring at the screen before him, but he had stopped clicking the buttons. He was listening now.

"I know these last few months haven't been easy on you. I know you miss our house and living close to your friends at school. I know it sucks that you had to stop Tae Kwon Do lessons, and that you're embarrassed to have your friends come over to Bubba's house and sleep over."

"We don't even have any good cereal, Mom," he finally said, and she lost it.

"I'm sorry. I. Am. So. Very. Sorry," she wept.

"Mom, hey Mom, it's okay. I don't need cereal."

"I didn't mean to lose it all. They took it from me. I—I can't begin to imagine what all of this has been like for you, baby. "

"Yeah, I miss the way it was, but mostly, I just want my mom back. I wanna kill those guys that hurt you," he said as he put his little face into his hands and started to cry.

"Come here," she said as she leaned in and pulled him to her.

"It's okay. It's all going to be okay. You'll see. I'm going to make it right. You'll see." The bench squeaked as he leaned into his mom.

Just then, Ziggy Baba leaped out again, sneak attacking them both from behind the curtains.

"That fucking cat," said the boy, and this time, she didn't say a thing.

"You know son, it's hard to see it now, but how you do anything is how you do everything. I am doing my best to show you how to navigate life's shittiest situations with grace and ease. It's not perfect, but I'm trying," she said, turning away from him to hide the tears now spilling down her face.

"Mom—when do you think this will all be over? When can I have my friends over again? Or order a pizza?" he asked.

"Soon buddy. Soon. I promise," she said, switching off the lights and grabbing her keys from the little hook next to the door.

"Come on—grab your stuff. It's time to go. Let's get you to Bubba's house now."

As a rule, the girl didn't drink and drive. It was lucky she had run out of wine the night before and had only been drinking iced teas and water all day.

"Get your things and get in the car. I'm taking you to Bubba's now," she told him.

The boy didn't answer her, but he shut off his Xbox and began to throw all his stuff into his backpack.

"And remember your controllers and your chargers, because if you forget anything, I am not bringing you back," she said, thinking of the gas money it was going to take to drive him all the way back. Shit. And then there were the toll roads. As she did the math in her head, she quickly realized that she would not be coming back. So, she poured out the rest of the kitty's food into a dish, filled his water bowl, and cleaned his litter box.

She put the rest of their food into her igloo cooler, shut off the propane to the trailer, and opened all the windows for the cat. Dilly would be home in 48 hours, and she couldn't afford to return, so it would have to do.

That long car ride back was hell. The boy sat in the back seat, clearly disturbed, and she worried about him flinging open the door and jumping out onto the highway, taking his life. That was how dark and serious he was acting after their talk.

My son is living in the backlash of Me Too too, she thought. She thought about all of his suffering and how this was larger than just what had happened to her. For the hundredth time, she thought about how these powerful men were hurting the little men too. And taking away their cereal.

As their crappy car climbed to the peak of the mountain, he said something that cut her to the core.

"I wish I had a different life," He said clearly.

"I mean, I love you mom, but . . ." He didn't finish the sentence, but he didn't have to. Tiny tears were now streaming down his cheeks too.

All her anger, all her pain flashed through her like a tsunami, the force breaking her heart in an instant. Tears poured down her face, making it hard for her to see the road ahead clearly.

This was it. This was her life. It was she who wanted to jump out from the moving car. It was *her* pain blinding herself on top of the mountainside. She was the one trapped inside, or rather they both were. As the girl fought to keep it all together, she heard a voice within repeat the phrase her grandmother had always said: "Per aspera ad Astra," which meant, "Through hardships to the stars,". She clung to these words, repeating them in her mind. *Per aspera ad Astra. Per aspera ad Astra. There has to be more to life than this*, she thought. *There just has to be . . .*

CHAPTER TEN

It's Meditation not Mediation You Asshole

A strange emotional limbo, a tangle of expectations, and the unknown with a touch of hearsay always surrounded settlements. There was no "unjustly done survivors club" or support workshop to dole out advice on how to deal with settlements, thus the solutions were often just as stressful as the initial offense. The girl had no adults around her capable of navigating this situation. Her mother was simply emotionally ill-equipped, and her father soldiered on. The aloneness intensified and she was forced to trust the council of her attorney, the Ogre, and the advice of her therapist and Dilly's mom, a romance novelist.

An email from her attorney arrived, informing her that on May 1, they would finally have their day in mediation with the judge. As this was her first time suing anyone, she had nothing to compare this experience to and was navigating uncharted territory. What she did know was that she was raped and wrongfully terminated, and as a consequence, her life and independence had fallen to shit. But sadly, there was no morality clause, and when bad men did bad things they were allowed to walk away. It was shitty and awful, but it had happened and the men who had done this to her, the men who had so casually taken away everything good in her life, would suffer. She rose for her day in court with a clear intention and prayed that her angels knew her intention and that the universe would hear her prayers.

She knew from recent experience that it was hard to set an intention to manifest what you truly wanted when you were operating from a place of fear. It was tricky to navigate manifestation when your fears posed actual threats to your health. Each thought and every breath had to become naturally conscious in order to activate and remain in the state of flow. And flow required trust. And trust meant that you had to surrender your power to the universe and your angels and be unwavering in your faith that the highest outcome for you was already on its way to you. Just waking up every morning being mindful was a level up from where she had been. Giving thanks to the universe and feeling grateful for every positive person, ability, and circumstances in her life from a sincere and pure heart, well, it had to be real. She had been through so much, and still felt she had magic within her, yet she had to be very pure and intentional about the intentions she was setting because of the heaviness that still filled her heart.

She left her son with her parents early that morning and set out to arrive at the legal building somewhere near Angel Stadium by 8:35 a.m.

It was a fancy corporate court, in an upscale hoity-toity office building. She was greeted kindly by a sleek blond lady, who looked like a greyhound wearing an expensive grey Nordstrom a- line skirt suit with a long-drawn face to match. The lady led the girl down several long posh corridors with deep fluffy carpeting.

"So, the other party and their attorneys have already arrived and are on the other side of the hall, so you shouldn't see them," she said as her long strides forward muffled her thin voice high in the air. "Here is the kitchen, we have stocked it with coffee, tea, soda, water, and snacks. At noon, a catered lunch will be delivered, and you can come out to help yourself here. The restrooms are down at the end of this hallway—and be advised, you share the same restrooms as the defendants."

Fucking great, thought the girl. She was on day one of her period and would have to visit the restroom frequently, increasing her chances of seeing one of them! Panic rose up in the girl's chest just as the woman finally opened a door up ahead and signaled for her to enter. There was the Ogre, red face peeking up over the top of his laptop, furiously typing away. He was on a call with his earbuds in and got off it just in time to greet his client.

"Hey there, tiger! Are you ready to get even today? How's my girl?" he asked, pushing himself back from the long conference table.

"Hello," she mumbled with a sad attempt for a smile as she entered this new space. She walked around to his side of the table and set down her purse and large overstuffed briefcase onto an empty chair.

"Did you know they are right next door to us?" she asked.

"I know, I know, that's just how these things work. But listen, don't worry, No one knows *which* room you are in and we will keep them away from you. You shouldn't have to see them today, unless you run into them in the hall or the bathroom. But that's not going to happen."

The girl wanted to believe him, but also knew she drank water like a camel and the probability of her needing to pee often was high, which meant she would have to pass by the door they all hid behind several times. Plus, she could already feel the blood leaking from her tampon out onto her pad. Her nerves were kicking into high gear, so she reached into her purse and took out a tiny piece of Xanax and chewed it.

"Don't you worry. Why don't you sit down and get comfortable? It's going to be a long day in there. Would you like some coffee or a bagel?"

"No thanks, I had my coffee and juice this morning before I left." The girl could barely breathe knowing that Big Global was just steps away down the hallway, so the thought of eating anything was out.

"It's real nice here! They are going to bring in a nice big lunch at noon, and you are going to need your energy up, so make sure you eat something, okay?" He meant well, but was annoying, nonetheless.

As the girl sat down, there was a helicopter that flew dangerously close to the large glass window wall as sirens burst from down below. *What now?* thought the girl. As the Ogre got up, he raced to the window to look down at the scene unfolding below. No one was coming for her; it was just the tail end of another carjacking in Anaheim.

The Ogre turned away from the window and began to describe how the day's events would unfold. He spoke very highly of the retired honorable judge who would be presiding over their case. She was she, so there was that, and in a matter of minutes, the judge entered the room to have a closed session review of the case, in all its details, as she understood it.

"Well, hello, my name is Sally, but you can call me Judge Sally or Your Honor," she said with a warm smile.

"I want you to know," Judge Sally continued, "that I understand this has been a very traumatic and terrifying event in your life and I am so very sorry for all you have been through."

The hot tears she had been holding inside began to flow freely. This was it—there was an accomplished, strong female judge who believed her. She hadn't known what to expect, but it wasn't this. The honorable Judge Sally leaned in toward her and held out a box of tissues, saying, "That's alright dear, you let it out. You let it all out. It's okay and you are safe here and they can't hurt you anymore."

It took the girl some minutes to get herself together and it was a nice touch that the judge reminded her of her favorite Aunt Susie.

"I knew I shouldn't have worn mascara today," she said.

They all laughed as the judge began reviewing facts of the case and occasionally asking for the girl to expand upon a statement or show her one of the many supporting documents, she had brought with her. The girl had come prepared; inside her briefcase was a folder containing photocopies of every incriminating text and email that her creepy boss had sent her, and one by one they were all seen by the judge.

The Ogre asked her to show Judge Sally her emails from her job promotion internal email announcement, as well as the texts wherein her boss asked her to meet him at his hotel and gave her the room number and address.

"We also have him on audio recordings, your honor," said the Ogre.

"When were these taken, and more importantly, were they taken with the knowledge of the defendant?" asked Judge Sally, looking suddenly stern.

"I took them on the night of my promotion meeting. It was customary for me to record all meetings in my role. What was different was my boss trying to have sex with me," said the girl, feeling braver now.

"Right, well just so you both know, I have him calling in from London here at 10:00 a.m. I need to get his side of the story as well," said the Judge.

This news wiped away any false sense of safety or camaraderie that the girl had felt up until now. The truth was that she was vulnerable and felt scared. Even knowing her perpetrator was over 7,000 miles away over a video connection still stuck fear in her. Her body tensed up and she stopped talking openly as she had been, and the judge noticed.

Judge Sally began again, "Listen. I can see you're upset. It is my job to hear both parties. That said, I have reviewed your case and I personally want to offer you my sincere condolences. What happened to you was not right and I am truly sorry for all you have been through. We are here today to see if we can make some of this right for you so that you can move on with your life now. Does that sound good?"

"Yes, Your Honor," said the girl as she blew her nose into a tissue.

The honorable Judge Sally stood up and walked around the table to a white board on the other side and picked up a colored marker in her hand.

"Now, I know that there is not enough money being offered today that can ever make what happened to you right. But we are going to try. Tell me, is there a number that is realistic, in your head, that you came here today with? Can you please tell me what that number is?" asked the judge.

The girl looked to her attorney, who was looking at her while nodding his head up and down, encouraging her to share her number with the judge.

"Well, um, yes, I feel that 1.3 million is where I want to start," she said, looking straight into the judge's eyes.

"I see. Well, I have no doubt that would work for you. However, in my experience, I can tell you right now, that this is a number that is not going to get us a successful agreement here today. But it is a starting point, and I am going to go next door and talk with them now," she said, exchanging a long look with the girl's attorney.

As the judge left the room, her attorney began talking quickly about how these things worked, and repeatedly emphasized how they "had a long way to go."

"It's going to be a long day, so get settled in," He repeated.

The girl wasn't sure what to think. Her guard was raised against all of them. Big Global, for obvious reasons, and against her attorney and the judge via her instinct.

While the judge was gone to meet the perp on a 10:00 a.m. call, the Ogre asked her to cue the audio recording to the most incriminating spots. She played and replayed various snippets of him compromising himself, verbally assaulting the girl, or straight out asking her for sex while telling her how amazingly beautiful she was. Together they marked down the times onto a legal pad and finished just before there came a knock on the door from the judge.

Judge Sally returned, stood in front of the whiteboard, and announced, "Well. He denied everything. Council? Your move."

"May I borrow your phone please?" he said to the girl.

"Your Honor, if you wouldn't mind, I would like to present this as evidence," he said as he pressed play and her boss's distinct British voice filled the room.

"Where's your bag? You're not staying overnight with me?" boomed the voice of the man who had just denied everything in front of Judge Sally only moments before.

"That's it!" said the Judge, and she was pissed.

"Council! You're coming with me! And bring that recording with you!" The judge was livid and turned on her heel, storming out of the room with the Ogre close behind, leaving the girl all alone.

The girl could tell that the judge didn't like being lied to and that Big Global's lies had just lost the war for them. From here, it was just a matter of how much and when.

Being in that fancy mediation room (that she ended up paying the bill for afterward) was like nothing she had experienced before. It was a little bit like buying a used car but having to pay to be on the showroom floor while a small troupe of acrobats danced and pranced and played around you. All while her painful memories were dredged up, not in the safety of her therapist's office, or her tiny dark bedroom where at least she could reach for a carafe of red wine or a pill with each triggering assault. There, she could openly reach for the vial in her purse and shake out a Xanax and a Norco to help take the pain away. Or she could have gone into the kitchen and made a plate of nachos to take back to her room and zone out to some Netflix series. Anything but sit here in this plush stuffy room, with just water, bad corner bakery catering, and a box of tissues to help ease her pain. She didn't dare nibble anymore of the zannie in her pocket, or she might not be able to drive home when it was time. If she ever got out of here.

No one had warned her that being in mediation would bring back every sexual violation, every unsafe moment in her life, every time she was touched inappropriately, treated with disrespect, laughed at by mean drunk boys, every time she was brave enough to tell but no one believed her, every possible infraction, every misogynistic moment—big or small—that had traumatized her in some way. The small moments when she didn't have a voice to speak up and say "Hey! You're hurting me! You are rubbing the skin off my knees and spine in this position. Please stop!" or "Hey! Stop ramming and jabbing your gross dry fingers up in me, it hurts and feels like you're cutting me." Every time a cock was jabbed and rammed with brute force down her throat, blocking her airway, she returned to that paralyzing anxiety deep within. All these fragmented moments from her past—from the collective past of every woman since the beginning of time—gathered around her neck, blocking her throat chakra, threatening to suffocate her with its weight. No one had prepared her for the onslaught of emotions and pain that would hang around her like an evil woolen scarf, threatening to suffocate her with its weight. There were so many parts of her life that were being brought in, only to be used against her in some fictitious and debaucherous way.

She didn't know when she had adopted the self-motto that she must be stoic and shoulder all of life's toughest moments alone. She wished she had brought someone with her. Her attorney had said that she could, but she thought against it and had even told Dilly, "No. Friends don't bring friends to sexual assault court." How wrong she was. Like so many events in her life, she had decided to go it alone and on some level was beginning to realize this pattern didn't suit her. Deep within her heart, she knew that denying all her feelings and not processing them and letting them come to surface was causing even deeper energy blockages that needed to be released. It was here in this bizarre court, of all places, completely alone, that she was forced into a speed-date scenario—encouraged to speak her truth about her most recent painful vicious acts, feel the emotions, cry about them in the instant in front of strangers, and move on in a matter of moments. The girl was in a sticky limbo, doing her best to navigate uncharted territories with her big girl panties on. She was not yet enlightened enough to remember that she was a spiritual being, having a physical experience, so her limitations were greater than her intuition which was buried underneath the day's events. There was so much unresolved stuff here for her to deal with, head on. On some deep level, she knew that all she needed was love and to end this saga, if only someone would give Judge Sally the memo.

For the next seven hours, over and over, the judge would leave and then re-enter the room, asking some more questions, pressing her for more details of the sordid encounters, and ultimately asking her for a lower number that the girl was willing to settle for, only to leave again.

This went on until it was almost 4:00 p.m. This time, when she entered it was different.

"We are at an impasse," Judge Sally announced, pacing the length of the room.

"We are too far away to reach a settlement, so I am going to apply my years of expertise and suggest a one-time best and final. You can either agree to it right now, and if they agree, this is done. I will draw up the paperwork and we will all be on our way. But this is a one-time offer. You will have ten minutes to determine if it is enough for you to move on with your life and continue to heal. If you say 'no', then we are finished here, and your attorney will receive my bill. If you should agree but they do not, we also have no deal. But, as it stands, we are just too far away to continue with this back and forth." As she stopped, she put the cap back onto the black marker and dropped it onto the table with a loud clack.

The girl looked at the white board, now scribbled with numbers on top that began with $1,300,000 and was now crossed out and re-crossed out and slashed alongside the day's negotiations. Down, down, down to 1.2, then 1.1, then one million, then to 850,000, then to 700,000, and on it went. Those were her tough and painstaking re-calculations under the close advisement of her attorney. There was much said, and the other side, in true Indian culture, only came up in tiny increments of $10,000 at a time. Insultingly small, like their size of their wee pricks, thought the girl.

The Ogre spoke up saying, "Look. This is not enough, it will never be enough, but we can end this now. You can ask for tax free, you can stipulate parameters, and I will consider reducing my fee if it will help you make the right decision and end this right now. This is a good deal. You were never going to get more than this. You need to take this deal," he said, smiling at her.

Well of course he was smiling at her! His third of her $300,000.00 would be a pretty penny easily earned for himself. After she paid him, and her therapist, and her student loans, and all her credit card debt, and after the hungry hands of her parents appeared outstretched, asking for back rent for the last year she had been with them, after, after, after, after a nice down payment on a new used car, she would barely have $40,000 in the bank as a life raft of savings to hold onto. It wasn't much. It wasn't enough. But Judge Sally and the Ogre made her feel, based on their expertise, that this was more than she should hope for. Together they convinced her that it was the right thing, to accept this amount and have the papers drawn up.

And so, after a long day negotiating and reliving the horrors of the last year, reluctantly the girl agreed. She was exhausted—mentally, spiritually, and emotionally. She had taken years off of the life span her heart could withstand, she was sure of it. She needed to release this toxic energy, to move on and to have closure. And so, it was with sorrow and an air of defeat that she weakly accepted the deal.

The judge left the room and returned in a matter of minutes with a smile, to announce that Big Global had accepted the deal too. Of course, they had. Assholes. When the Judge returned, she also extended the apologies of Big Global's council. How ironic. The lead council was a bitter woman that the girl had known of only in elevators and in passing at HQ. This ox-like woman had remained steadfast in her defense of the bastards and then finally, finally at the end, admitted guilt and extended her apologies? It was too little too late, and the girl thought that she could shove her apologies right up her tight ass. She left them to themselves and began the paperwork. She returned and began to review all of the stipulations. Because the girl was over a certain age, the money would have to be held in a trust for an extra 30 days. And because of this or that, there would be long delays that would have the girl questioning if they would even honor their shitty lowball promise. Hence the painstaking waiting period to receive the settlement.

The day of mediation, she was on one of the heaviest flows of her life. She had to excuse herself and walk up out of that room and down the long hall to change her tampon and shove another maxi pad into the lining of her panties. She was releasing and shedding the skins of so much trauma. She was weak from the emotions, the heavy loss of blood, and the psychological and spiritual purging and cleansing. When she was finally free to walk down to her car, she felt something new. For the first time in a long time, the girl felt gratitude well up within her. She needed to meditate and promised to give herself the gift of silence and peace of mind as soon as she got home. In the days that would follow, when people in the world would ask how she was, she would reply, "Grateful. I am grateful, thanks, how are you?" It was the best she had felt in years. When she went home that night, she opened a bottle of $3.99 wine and celebrated her victory against Big Global, her strength, her vision, and her future. Bloody cheers.

She had absolutely no clue as to how frustrating the process of settling really was. What this really meant was that you settle on your values. You settle on what you know you are owed versus what you are willing to take to make it all go away. At some point along the way, you realize that all the tiny moments of stress in the ER, in the shower, in bed hungover, all this time was stolen from you too. You realize you will never get this back. That no amount of money, no promises, no apologies will ever bring that back. As the gem is revealed, you now know that time and health are the most precious commodities you will ever have.

CHAPTER ELEVEN
Waiting Games

In life, you only know what you have experienced before, and there was no sexual violation pay out club for the girl to lean on. She had no idea that the long hellish day of court would lead to almost another 90 days of more stress than ever before, wondering if she would live long enough to ever see a penny of her money.

Meanwhile, she operated as if all would soon be normal. She opened up three new folders on her laptop: Travel, Home, and Car. She frequented Zillow for available rentals closer to her son's school, cars that would last her a decade and not kill her back yet were still safe enough to teach her son how to drive in, and bargain furnishings she could assemble herself, once they found a home. The third file was her dream file. She read up on exotic travel destinations, signed up for airfare watch alerts, and collected clippings on baths of Cambodia, walls of the Northern Lights in Oslo National Park, and jungle retreats in Brazil, Peru, and beyond.

The Imaloya Institute looked good, but then again, so did Maui. Her files grew bigger and bigger, filled with the dream shopping spree she was entertaining. This was better than Netflix and, and on top of it all, she was sober! For the most part, she was getting up and through her days without the crushing panic and debilitating anxiety keeping her spirit down. This "dream shopping" was a solid distraction and a good use of time as they were going to be starting over. They needed a fresh start filled with beds, bed linens, furnishings. She began keeping files of discounts and looked at the calendar for upcoming holiday sales.

Their car was about ready for the graveyard and just in time. So, she searched for organizations she could donate it to that were capable of fixing it up and giving it to someone in need. Files and files of stuff they needed were created based on the promise of the settlement coming through. It was fake spending, but it was fun.

The girl daydreamed about her money until she was always interrupted by the reality of what she actually would receive and what it must go toward. First of all, she would pay off any existing debts she had. Next, she would put enough into savings and investments that would assure she would NEVER find herself in a similar position for the rest of her life. Then, she would reach out to Djedi again and invite him to join her—she would find them a new place to live, buy herself a new car, take them on a proper holiday, and get on with her life.

Yet, at the same time, she feared the money. She had never had good money examples in her life and was afraid she would blow it all. This was her deepest fear, and she was scared. She needed to instill some safeguards, like bumper lanes in a kiddy bowling alley for herself. Did they even do that? Was the banking and financial services industry smart enough to set up kiddy parameters for newbies of moderate wealth? No clue. She would just have to have some financial conversations with savvy people around her and do her best. Lord knows she would need to redefine her thoughts around money, so she bought the "You are a badass at making money" book as a best effort and prayed for the best.

In reality, the first thing she did was buy her son some cereal, planned a sleepover with pizza. She made a promise to herself that she would stop consuming meat. It no longer served her, and she knew it was time to raise her vibration. There was more she wanted to do: open her own company, write a novel, plan a trip to Hawaii, and live happily ever after. Or at least get woke.

But as the days passed and the date of her payday grew closer, the girl's intuition caused a slight panic within. Her intuitive self-sensed that something was going to block her from receiving her settlement as she was promised. Sure enough, this tiny fear at the corner of her mind grew, and whether it was a case of the fear manifesting and becoming the reality or her lightening up returning her to the flow of her own psychic abilities, she couldn't be sure. All she knew was that the day on the calendar, 30 days after her long mediation day, came and went with no call, no communication from her lawyer . . . nada.

The girl's mind began to race in a blind panic, as she frantically asked Uncle Google to answer all of her deepest fear-based questions. Akin to googling heart attack symptoms when your upper left arm or jaw hurt, the girl knew she was spiraling out of control. Mania quickly consumed her; she began calling the Ogre's office, leaving messages, and sending long emails to him and his assistant Angel, trying to learn what was happening. Why had everyone gone silent and where was her fucking money?! They had to pay, right? Big Global had to honor the paperwork that she and Judge Sally had signed and had given her a copy of, right? What would happen if they didn't make the deposit into her attorney's trust fund? What then? What would she do? What then? *What if?*

She wasn't fine, far from it. She was pretending to be "fine" just like every woman who ever said they were feeling "fine" was feeling, which to this girl meant she was feeling *fucked!* Fine was just a four-letter word that began with an F. *Go disappoint the next bitch, I'm busy*, she thought. So, instead of sitting alone in her room mulling over this, she decided to go for a walk. A hawk walk.

When she returned, she sat down and wrote another email to the Ogre. She could see from his social media account that he was off playing in Joshua Tree with his wife for the weekend. Never mind that she was waiting for news about this—the biggest event in her life, but yeah, go ahead and make bonfires and ride quads. *Moronic*, thought the girl selfishly. How dare anyone go on living their best life, while she was stuck inside in a waiting game of hell?

Her words slipped, causing her to rectify them, casting reverse Point of Creation/Point of Destruction or POC/POD charms and incantations multiple times daily. Every hour that passed by felt like another year to her. Impatience grew exponentially and was magnified by the unknown and heightened by her instinct. She experienced more stress *these* days than she had immediately after the rape. This would be impossible for most people to understand, but fortunately for her, her inner circle consisted of only "not most people."

Her tribe was small, and she was good with that. The simple truth was, as she grew older, friends she had known as lifers for 30 years or more held nothing in common with her anymore. She felt a closeness with new people who had done the same work she had and found themselves vibrational matches. Her tribe consisted of beautiful quality people who she might have only known for a minute. Yet here they were, bright, light, and given carte blanche and a hearty "Welcome to my world" from the girl. There was no reason to keep the negative energy around those old-timers who sucked the life out of her or who were trapped in their own never-ending dramas. Hers became a quiet and simple life. This also meant that in times of trouble, like this past year, that she was mostly alone and not surrounded by people with any experience navigating life circumstances like this. And while she felt glad that they hadn't suffered like she had, she also felt alone.

Growing up, she had lacked any concrete examples of how to manage healthy relationships, how to be responsible with money, or how to be emotionally healthy, and she could see it clearly now. How there was a disconnect between the love her parents had for her and the teachings they provided. She never meant to make anyone responsible for her happiness. There was no fault, no blame in this statement—rather, merely facts. It was a coming-of-age moment for the girl as she realized that she must always choose to take accountability and responsibility instead. That this was the way of the advanced warrior spirit. This was using intellectual power plus the power of love. As a parent herself, it became increasingly important to her that she led her son by example, providing best use cases in life to provide for him and give him any advantage.

She sat for a while and thought about this version of what tomorrow's better man might look like. He would do no great harm to this man. He would be a gentle warrior, not a genital warrior like men of the past. The man of tomorrow would embrace his divine feminine and be gentle, calm, and kind. A man who knew how to fish in the digital age, who could code and raid but chose to keep such skills to the game.

Lately when she looked at her son, she saw a growing child with some evidence of deep emotional damage. This scared her, as she was likely the cause of all his love, light, and health, but also this hurt and the shadows. Along the way, somehow, in-between the babe popping out of her vagina without an owner's manual and her best intentions, she shat the bed just a little. The thing was, she wanted to make sure she made enough time to listen closely to him so that they could avoid any permanent damage and grow through it, into a stronger bond. Ideally. She just wanted to check in and see if the boy was in any deep emotional pain. She wanted to talk about it with him and see what could be done together to release it and improve the way she was feeling about him today. The boy-man she saw before her was strong, smart, sensitive, funny, kind, brave, and capable. But also … a teenager. And there was damage on that path no matter who you were.

There were things she wanted to say to Vinyl, like "Son, I want to teach you to wear comfy warm things that bring you joy in the cold months and to not give a frick what anybody thinks. I want you to continue to be the guy who carries in all the heavy stuff from the car, opens doors, and takes responsibility for himself in all the micro and macro ways. I want you to keep finding solutions to help people you may never meet. Keep being mindful about the effect your decisions today will have on tomorrow. May you always have the strength to find your voice and use it during tough situations. And send all enemies LOVE, because LOVE—not fear—is the key to everything. Yours and mine. What's yours is mine. Your love is mine and my love is yours and you are my greatest love." But these perfect words only seemed to find themselves in her thoughts when she was lying in bed late at night without a pen or keyboard to capture them.

So, this was it. Day after day after day she would wake up, and go through the motions, eating less meat, drinking less alcohol, and swallowing fewer pills. A shift was about, which came with the spring. Her job was to live long enough to get them out, set them up, and maintain a happy and secure life for them both. Her job was to ensure that she would never, ever find herself in a position like this again, for the rest of her life. And if she could inspire or help some people struggling with the very same traumas along the way, well then, it would have been a life worth living. To allow meaning to grow out of trauma was a core vision for the girl. It was bittersweet, but she held on to this as it resonated in her body, mind, and soul.

It wasn't easy showing up for herself and typing all the words into the computer, rehashing her pain every single fucking day. She would have rather hit a joint and caught a sunset on the sand anywhere, but she believed in reaching one free hand down in life to lift up other people who were struggling below.

These were the thoughts that filled her mind in-between looking for rentals closer to her son's school. It was hard not to check her emails obsessively, looking for any sign of her funds coming through. Unfortunately, no emails came into her; she would do her best to be patient but not hearing anything prompted her to initiate emails to her council and ask where the fuck her money was in the nicest possible way. He would give her a frustrating reply, telling her to be patient, which drove her crazy, when her instincts and deep fears were screaming at her from within.

This naughty cacophony blasted her daily, never letting up. Over and over, it rang in her head, buzzing like an annoying fly she just couldn't kill. It was perpetual in its assholery and annoying as fuck. Bless and release. Bless and release. Bless and release, she thought and said and meant. And so, slowly, she started going out into the world and doing the things that lit her soul on fire. She went out into the world unafraid to look at an apartment with a male agent, without the fear of being attacked. She slowly stopped sending ice daggers to men who looked at her in Starbucks or on her morning walks. She stopped imagining how she could best smash in their trachea or gouge out an eyeball, and instead just nodded her head in that old academic way and moved on. She stopped ordering a hot water to go, in case she needed to throw it in the face of some perv messing with her on the way out. She stopped drinking from glass bottles in case she needed to smash it alongside the curb and shove it into a man's jugular. Eventually, her rape mindset shifted as she allowed some softer thoughts to occupy her capable mind.

In return, the world seemed to notice and responded kindly. She got a contract position. Then another. The money that came in helped to ease her mind and aid her in a shift out of fear and desperation and into confidence and generosity once again. She wrote a lovely letter to prospective landlords, explaining any dips—well, more like landfills—in her credit scores and compensated with her character, her references, and her checkbook. This led to multiple acceptance offers and gave her new decisions to make. "Let's go make some good choices," she said to herself.

There was just one thing she wanted to do first . . .

There was a little girl in her son's class, who had stolen his heart the day they met. Emmie was her name, and she was a very special girl, but also one deep in pain. The girl could see some of herself as a little girl in this child. There is a certain somber silence that is carried in the eyes of little girls who have seen terrible things. There is an ominous code of silence that they feel they need to fall into in order to protect themselves and the ones they love. They do this, not knowing any better. They do this thinking they are doing the smart, brave thing—the only thing they can do. But what they don't know, can't possibly know, is that there are others, elders like the girl, out there who can see right through them.

This experienced vision comes with great responsibility. They can see the lies they think they must tell. They can hear the cries in their silence. They can see the frown lines in their resting faces, and more than that, they can sense the pain they identified with at some point along their own beaten path.

She saw herself in the girl, the sadness reminding her of how her favorite Aunt Susie would often reflect upon what a beautiful but deeply sad child she had been. How the eyes told it all and how she was shocked that no one had ever checked in deep enough to get to the root of her adolescent despair. There was something of this in Emmie too. The girl within in her knew she needed help. She heard the lies and saw what the world couldn't or wouldn't for many years, if ever.

She had a painting in her room, a favorite from her days in University; it simply said, "She thought She could, and so She did." The small light pink portrait reminded her of the little girl within who had healed along the way, and she knew it would be perfect for Emmie. So, she wrapped it in last season's Fab Fit Fun box and put some other cool things in there that a teenage girl would want. Some new lip gloss, a bracelet, some crystals, a candle, and the painting. She drove it to school and gave it to Emmie's mom before the kids got out of school one day. It was a good thing she did so, because Emmie's parents took her out of their school the following month. Emmie would not be returning, which led to heartbreak for her son and more growth opportunities. It stung but was manageable. Anything was, really, with the right mindset.

She felt more like herself than she had in a while. It was time for a shower, to keep moving, to transform, follow the butterflies, find the hawks, and be the rivers.

In the shower, instead of reliving the hell of her rape, she thought about how as a young teen, she had been promiscuous by default. You see, the girl had lost her virginity one night, by her babysitter—a common occurrence—when she was only five years old.

At a sleepover on the night of her 13th birthday, her two best friends had a hoe "intervention" with her:

"You know we love you, right?" said Carrie Ann, standing close by on the chalk-covered sidewalk in the front of her driveway, as the girls waited for the sun to set so they could go toilet paper a house and run amok through the park.

"Sure, I love you guys too!" said the girl, fiddling with the Panasonic radio dials, trying to get Madonna's voice to come in clearly.

"We, um, well, the thing is, there is something we want to talk to you about, and it's pretty serious," said Irini, the girl from Greece, whose name meant peace.

"Uh-huh, it's cool. I'm here, aren't I? Just say it already," she said as she stood with her weight leaning back, sticking one hip out to the side with her hand on it.

"Okay, well, you know how on early days when we all go to Nick's after school for pizza?"

"Yeah, so?" snapped the girl while chewing her big wad of Hubba Bubba gum.

"Well, the thing is, while we all get obnoxious and have fun inside the restaurant, you and some of the boys disappear out back in the alleys and there's talk. People are saying you are blowing some of the guys back there."

"That's such bullshit! You know what? This party is over. That's right, you heard me. Just go call your mommies to come pick you up. I can't believe you two. Ganging up on me like this, and on my birthday? This is so unfair," the young girl pouted.

"Listen up, we care about you and we love you. We know there's something bigger going on with you, and we're not saying this to hurt you. We just want you to know how much we love you and that we thought you might, um, want to think about these things and maybe, like, um, maybe try to not to anymore, if you know what I mean?" This was Carrie Ann, the logical one of the three.

The girl honestly can't remember what was said next, but she did remember that the party went on. They bonded even closer than ever and still managed to toilet paper the park, stay up until 3:00 a.m., and freeze Stacy's underwear in Tupperware. That was her 13th birthday. Since then, she had been more aware of herself as she embarked upon a lifetime's journey to clear herself of this taboo sexual energy.

In the days to come, she finally got an email from the Ogre, outlining her upcoming payday. In it, he explained how the funds would need to be deposited into his trust first, and from there he would cut her a check and she could come pick it up at his office. This news brought her great relief and she made plans to take Vinyl out that night to celebrate.

She fished through her purse, digging for her skinny wallet, and came up with $54.00 and a credit card with about $40 more available, and that was it. Well, she thought, she could just eat an apple to fill herself up first and take him out for dinner and she would just watch him enjoy himself.

"Hey Vinyl, grab your hoodie and throw on some flip flops, let's get you some poke and catch a movie at the bargain theatre tonight."

"Awesome, Mom! Thanks! Just let me finish this round," he said, looking up with a smile.

This kid is always finishing a round, she thought, as she realized the round she was about to be finishing as soon as she got paid and left all this behind her.

She grabbed some crackers and an apple, poured some wine into a mason jar for the movies, and threw it all into a bag in her purse.

Once at the poke restaurant, the boy scooted into a booth and she sat with her back to the line. They played really good music here, as Stevie Wonder mixed into Massive Attack into Chaka Khan. The girl was loving it and was in a joyful mood and it showed, as she sat-danced in her chair, watching her son enjoy his extra-large poke bowl. The latest Star Wars movie was still in theaters and they were going to make a quick run by Walmart after his dinner to buy cheap candy before enjoying the film together. She was trying to decide if they had enough for candy, a box of cereal, milk, and a bottle of wine, when she was startled by her son's rude tone.

"MOM! STOP it NOW! You're embarrassing me!" he hissed.

Unaware that there were three young cute girls in the line standing behind her, her stomach ached, like a kick in the gut as she looked back at him with incredulous eyes.

"Excuse me? What did you just say to me?" she asked the boy in a hushed tone.

"I mean it, Mom! You are embarrassing me!" he spat.

Clearly hurt, as she sat here in what was supposed to be a celebratory moment, she was not eating so that he could, and now this? *Oh, hell no*, thought the girl.

"Really? I'm embarrassing you. Well! I wouldn't want to embarrass you, so you go on and enjoy your dinner alone. I'll be waiting out in the car."

She got up with tears in her eyes and got out of the poke place just as more hot tears rolled down and over her cheeks. She really wasn't clear on what she would do, as her hurt was overriding all logic. She knew he didn't deserve to go to the movies—that he deserved a consequence—and that she had to get it together and make this a teachable moment. But how? What was the right thing to do? She just didn't have an instant easy answer. So, she just sat there and prayed. She prayed to her ancestors, to her angels and guides, to God of all creation, and to the universe to give her the right words to say when he got in the car.

She had no idea how much time had passed when he finally appeared, walking in a slow shuffle toward her in the car. She knew by his body language that he knew he was in trouble and was waiting for the other shoe to drop.

"Vinyl, what was that back there?"

"Mom, there were lots of people behind you and your dancing and singing was embarrassing me. Everyone was staring. Like, everyone," he said, squirming in his seat.

"Ohhhh were they? I guess they were. I guess they were all looking at me like, 'Oh! Look at that cool Mom over there who is going without a meal again so that her child can eat.' Or were they looking at my dope moves? Was that it, son? Was that why they were all looking at me? And also, since when have I ever cared about what other people—strangers we will never see again this lifetime—think about me? Oh, hell no! Me? I am your mother and I work my ass off to give you everything I can. It may not be enough at times, and it's far from perfect, but make no mistake, mister, it is always the best I can do for you. But I embarrassed you? Well excuse the fuck out of me, then." With that, she started the car, reverted into a stony silence, and drove across the street to Walmart.

She didn't have a plan, beyond knowing that they needed some more cereal and milk for him, and now all the wine she could afford for herself. She still hadn't decided what to do about the movies. Clearly, he didn't deserve to go. So, she grabbed a small shopping basket and a sanitizing wipe and wiped it down. She was still praying when she stopped on the bread aisle, next to the wines. When something caught her eye. There before her were the cutest little pies she had ever seen. What more, they were only 50 cents. An idea came to her in a flash and she put two peach pies, a lemon, and a blueberry into her cart. She raced to grab a bottle of red wine, then ran over to the cereal aisle, and finally to the dollar candy. She had a smile back on her face as a plan took shape in her mind. She raced through the self-checkout and walked back out to the car. There sat Vinyl in the front seat, playing a game on her phone.

She opened the back car door behind him and threw in her shopping bags. She bent over to fish out two of the pies, then closed the door and rapped on his window hard.

"Step out of the car son. NOW," she said intensely.

"No way, Mom. I'm not coming out"

"Son, you open up this goddamn door this instant or Lord help you, this won't go well for you."

The boy looked up at her with fear. He knew he had gone too far.

"Son, I'm not asking, I'm telling. You get out and stand up and face me right here, right now."

Scared but knowing he was wrong, he knew he had it coming and that if he ignored her, it would end up ten times worse, so he put down her phone and got out of the car.

"Look at me, Vinyl. Look me in the eyes. What do you see? I'll tell you. You are looking at your mother. The one person on this planet who loves you unconditionally, even when you kick me in the gut and tear my heart out like you did back there. Now. Do you know how much that hurt me back there? And from you? I don't need that from you son . . . and for what? Because you say that I embarrassed you. You know what we're going to do? We're gonna have a pie fight, right here in this parking lot. And it will probably get filmed and posted on your precious YouTube or Tok-tok or Insta. And THAT—that shit is going to be embarrassing. You don't know what embarrassing is. Oh no. That's right. Because what you did back there? You tried to kill my sunshine. And let me tell you—*NOBODY* KILLS MY SUNSHINE! SO, let's go!" she said, handing him a peach pie.

"No Mom! No! I'm sorry! I won't ever kill your sunshine again," he wailed.

"Please Mom, please! I don't want to fight with you. I'm sorry, I'm so sorry. I won't ever do it again," he cried.

"How do I know you won't? How can I be sure?" she asked, calming down now, lowering her raised pie arm down from her attack stance.

"I promise. I'm sorry," he wailed.

"I believe you are, my son. I believe you are," she said as she pulled him into a bear hug there in the middle of the bustling parking lot.

"Now, you can apologize, that's needed. But don't ever say you are 'sorry.' Saying 'I'm sorry' is a negative psychological connotation that affirms to the grid—to the universe—that you are indeed a sorry individual, and nothing is further from the truth. Just apologize and let's go see if we're not too late to catch this movie."

"You mean, we still get to go?" he asked, looking up to her with his wise, wide blue eyes.

"I mean it. I believe you will never do that again. And if you do? You know what fate awaits you."

"Pie fight!" they both said at the same time, laughing.

As they turned to get back into the car, Vinyl asked her, "But Mom—just one thing. Can we eat the pies?"

"Get in the fucking car," she said with a smile as she started it up as NWA's "Fuck the Police" came on.

CHAPTER TWELVE
The Big Payback

"It was all a dream, I used to read Word Up! magazine." Biggie's melodic voice filled her earbuds as she danced around the house, packing and fully embracing her sunshine. It felt good to dance again, and to be packing instead of panicking was a welcome bonus too.

On the day her funds were transferred from her attorney's trust account into her designated checking account, she took the family out to dinner and they celebrated with a nice bottle of wine. No sooner had they said "Cheers!" when her father turned the conversation to the amount, he "figured" she owed them for staying with them over the last year.

She felt torn - outraged on the one hand but understanding. She felt sorry for the shell of a man that used to be. Once strong in body, mind and spirit, since retiring to a small merry go round life of walking, watching too much news, golf, and his dog, the blah of the rinse repeat, well, she could understand him wanting to be in on a little of this excitement. They had extended small loans to her and of course she was going to make it right. It was poor timing. She tuned him out for a minute and tried to enjoy their nice meal out together, the one she was paying for with years taken from her life. She shuddered at the greedy hands of friends and family members, ones she never saw coming, holding their fat palms outstretched to her in a cheap give me, give me, give me manner. No wonder she had blockages and issues around money that she would heal in the near future.

She looked around the table and thought - *fuck it. If he needs it now, he needs it. Just please make him shut the fuck up and leave me alone so we can enjoy this peace I am feeling, then so be it.*

Then came her mother, then her attorney's lion's share cut, and her therapist, and her doctors, and more specialist vendors, and forensic experts who had transcribed the audio files from her devices. The student loans, the investments, savings for taxes, and Roth IRAs. Together they formed a serpent-shaped conga line, each tapping their feet, impatiently demanding checks.

By the time she had paid everybody off, some of her student loans, and her debts, and secured a car and new housing with their new beds and furnishings and on and on and on, she locked away as much of it as she could into IRAs and solid annuities and savings. Her daily checking dropped back down to a happy normal amount. After $18,000 to the forensic psychologist, $10,000 to Dad, and on and on, her momentary feeling of *I'm rich!* quickly faded into *OH MY GOD LOOK HOW MUCH IS GONE AND WHERE DID IT ALL GO???*

But she was grateful and needed to get busy living her new life. After months of stress and anxiety and fear eating away at her heart, sabotaging her nerves and giving her a limited horizon, she was finally in a good place and rising. AHO! Positive change was coming her way and she couldn't have felt more grateful.

She was grateful to her son for his confidence in her during rocky times, she was grateful for her team—Dilly, the Ogre, her therapist, herself, her healers at the HOMA ranch, and to her angels, ancestors, and guides for leading her through dark times. There was just one last entity she needed to cast her gratitude toward in a genuine light, and that was her perpetrators. This was the hardest fucking thing to do, and she wasn't even sure she could do it, but, alas . . . she had to give it her best effort.

Life had taught her some years ago that survival demanded forgiveness. After some years of adopting the words and then the actions of "bless and release," she was finally able to develop a natural rhythm for this best practice as it became semi-automatic. In life, when dark people or dark energies or dark circumstances would surround her, she would survive, reflect, forgive, and eventually . . . bless and release. Now understand, it was a million times easier said than done and still fucking hard as a meteor. But it was absolutely necessary to carry on with one's life without being completely destroyed. This was the gig. The minute details that came and went, the tragedies that triggered, the events and assaults and insults and deep heart digs, well, they would always come again in another person, in another time. The best you could do was prepare yourself, ascend yourself, shield yourself, and the key to all of it, forgive yourself first and come second to none.

She realized she needed to forgive herself first and to understand that *she had done nothing to deserve the awful attack that happened to her.* It was *them,* not her. More importantly, she needed to understand that she had the power over them to forgive them. So, she decided to raise her voice and use her internal goddamn megaphone. She had to forgive them in order to move on. To truly be free. To ascend, she had to truly heal and not just stuff it and pretend. She had to be able to be in the world and see the brand and still live her best life.

Which meant that, against all odds, she needed to forgive them all. The babysitter when she was five, the punk rocker at 22, and the assholes of Big Global today. Like a cheap clearance sale, all of them had to go.

She blessed and she released, and she shook her ass to the beats that filled her heart and ears as the music pulsed, and she moved around their rooms packing up everything in reusable plastic tubbies, carefully labeling everything with masking tape and a thick black sharpie.

The girl's humor returned as she labeled random boxes "butt plugs" for her amusement. She hired movers and signed a lease agreement. She drove a brand-new car and was offered "wealth management" counseling from the tellers at her bank, who now looked at her with awe and respect. It was stupid, really. How many years had the stress taken from her life essence? Everything she was about to do was temporary, while the scars within her would remain.

Bless & Release

She booked airfare through the summer and secured accommodations. She bought two new Cal King mattresses with all the goodies and some new fantasy furniture from her pre-arranged files. She entered into contracts, negotiated, ordered, emailed, called, and orchestrated the next chapter of her life. It was time, and she was moving onward and upward.

The price of her ascension was steep and given the chance she would not ever do it again, but she had made it. She was going to be alright—better than alright—and vowed never to allow herself to be in such depths again. Indeed, trauma was strange and terrifying as it could come in an instant and wipe out everything you thought you had. Yet, from this point on, she would be armed with her angels, ancestors, and guides. She would have a healer network to run to, her altar, her safe place, her womanhood, her HOMA, and her home.

She had always wanted to wear a long sheer white cape lined with gold satin or silk with a big, oversized hood on it. It would hide the sides of her face and her chin as she aged and walked wisely though life, strong in her decisions and proud of her experience and wisdom.

Their new house had all-white marble floors, with walls of windows letting in the light, looking over a lake surrounded by a green park and gazebo below. A single crystal hung from the apex of the window which was why the girl took the space. As it turned out, the previous tenant had been an energy worker and crystal healer who decided to cash it all in and go to live in a tiny house in Alaska.

As the long summer days lazily rolled by, the girl got skinnier and skinnier, transforming herself in the sweet summer sun. In her new life, it was as if every traumatic imprint that had held her back from her best self before had been lifted and the blessings rolled in. Her new neighbors were lovelier than she ever could have imagined. Life was not perfect, and there were small disappointments that came in time, but nothing—truly nothing—could or would rock the core of this new woman.

There was one very specific item that the girl had gotten for her son. Well, aside from his new gaming PC they built together and his deluxe gaming desk and the trip to Maui. There were so many good things in their lives, but the biggie was their new puppy.

After everything they had been through, they both agreed that they needed some purebred Golden Retriever puppy love in their lives. And that was how they met Bluefin.

She did her research and found a breeder of champion pups in Lake Lanier, just outside of Atlanta, Georgia. So, she bought a round trip ticket, put down a deposit over the phone, and let her son pick out the pup from a picture sent via email. The puppy was adorable. They met on a front porch in the lazy Georgia countryside, early on a hot summer morning. He got nervous on the car ride back to the airport and shit the bed, or the cage, quite literally. The girl called the breeder, calculated the time until their flight departed, and made a U-turn in the middle of the highway.

They raced back where the nice heavyset woman in jean cutoffs and a dirty t-shirt was waiting for them with a hose, some towels, new bedding and a shot of an anti-motion-sickness remedy for the pup. Now in serious jeopardy of missing their flight, the next hour and a half were straight out of a movie. Driving against trains, running and racing through airports nonstop with a puppy in one arm and her inhaler clutched in her other hand, hearing her name being paged for final boarding alerts over the airport's sound system, and being the last one allowed on the plane before they cross-checked and pulled back from the gate.

During the long flight home, the adorable puppy looked up at her, his head just peeking out of the top of his new soft nylon carrier at her feet. She reached her hand down and smoothed his face in long loving strokes, which would continue to be a signature soothing move between them. She thought she had gone to get the puppy for her son, but it quickly became apparent that teenagers who thought they wanted a forever dog fell short on the extra responsibilities part, and so, she ended up with her own service dog. The truth was, she needed that dog in her life and they both needed some sweet, sweet joy.

It was a good thing too, for upon her arrival home, the average daily balance of her bank account left her in need of a service animal. It was astounding, really, how much the hands that demanded had collectively taken from her alleged "big win." There was nothing big about it. However, it was enough to provide a healthy start over, a re-do, and this was what she did.

She was beyond generous with her friends, with her son, and with their friends. She bought her first BBQ and learned to grill (and how to clean a grill). She went ocean kayaking in shark reefs where they snorkeled. She swam deep under rainbows, having goddess mornings under gentle trade winds and rainbows with dear friends. She was able to create incredible healthy, whole-food, plant-based meals that brought her much joy. There were lots of little moments that added up to a beautiful six months of relaxation, birdsong, and piña coladas, before she actively got back into the flow of the daily grind.

The difference this time was that she had so many options, as if it was being orchestrated for her by a magical presence. It wasn't ever going to be a grind again. She had seen to it and would do everything she could to keep this peaceful feeling growing deep within her. She had discovered the secret to life was simply making the decision to "Be happy *now*," and so it was.

CHAPTER LUCKY THIRTEEN

Ascension

The power of never giving up was real as fuck. Her perseverance had brought her to a place where a Nyika crystal hung from the apex of the 60-foot cathedral ceilings that met windows facing the bright blue open sky against the vivid green banana trees that filled her new backyard. A white light space emitted a calm feeling in this garden, giving her hope and a great space to begin again. She was aware that not everyone got such a chance and was determined to do her very best with this blessed opportunity.

For all she had been through, she had learned a thing or two. She had learned to trust the wait. She learned to trust that she was being prepared for her blessings. In order to receive them, she had to be *ready* to receive them, and this was a tough lesson to learn. The day finally came when she was able to see that the things she had gone through were not random at all. In the end, she believed that everything you went through grew *you*. It was learning how to trust the process that eventually allowed her to level up. Living in a new home where she could apply new lessons to her new chapter in life was just what she needed.

Her son called her from his new room upstairs, "Hey Mom! Mom, what time is the internet guy gonna get here?"

"Between one and three, but I love you without the internet too," she called back as she thought about the power of being connected versus the power of choosing to remain disconnected.

"Don't go changing, to try to please me . . ." she sang.

"Mom, seriously! Please don't sing anymore!" he said, bounding down the stairs and barging into the kitchen heading toward the refrigerator. He swung back the door and stared into the neat rows of coconut water, sparkling water, and bottled water. She was into hydration and it showed.

"Where did you put the spicy chips?" he asked sweetly.

"There are none. You finished them and you have to eat something healthy. Have some fruit, or I can make you a smoothie if you want?"

"Ugh. Not another one of your protein shakes. I hate it when you put all your stuff in them. They taste chalky. Like powder. Gross."

"You know what's totally gross? Colon-rectal cancer in your thirties because you didn't eat enough fiber and chalk growing up. That's it, chip-chop! Hand me a cup of ice please," she said, grabbing a banana and her supplement canisters from the cupboard.

"I swear if you make me drink that I'm gonna puke!" said the boy dramatically.

"And I swear, one day when you're way ahead of the game and not going through actual food withdrawals, when the entire planet has decided it can only consume chalky shakes to support the 11 billion inhabitants of which I'm not one of, you will thank your spirit mother who prepared you by weaning you off of pizza, meat, and spicy chips today. You're welcome, my love," she said, handing him a mason jar filled with a sweet summer smoothie.

Moving in was well orchestrated, thanks to the professionals she paid to do all the heavy lifting. Rebuilding was a process that required one specific skill . . . assembly. In the literal sense, there was a PC, furniture, and two lives to rebuild, and while the girl had skills, assembly wasn't one of them. So, she called a buddy from University to come help her. Slowly over the next three days, beds were delivered, and tables and chairs and lamps were built as things eventually found their place. It felt good to finally have a place of her own again and she enjoyed decorating the house with the intention that Djedi would finally get to come and join them.

She chose the right side of everything—the divine feminine side of the bed—giving Djedi the side closest to the door, so he could protect her from any unwanted intruders. She hung her Native American oil painting on his side and placed her small antique dresser next to the bed, leaving its two small drawers empty for him to use when he arrived. Likewise, in the bathroom, she chose her vanity and placed her cosmetics and things around the sink she preferred, leaving the other for him. Her intentions brought him into the space, filling it slowly with love, little by little, with each decision she made.

Together, she and her son worked side-by-side, creating a space he was incredibly proud of. She loved seeing him take pride in what she had rebuilt for them. Especially since it had been a long time since he had felt like having friends over. They ordered all the parts to build a gaming PC together, and they built it from scratch together. Then came his massive gaming desk and refrigerator, as they co-created such an amazing room for him that he wanted to be in it all of the time. He was happy here and it showed. He was doing better in school than ever before. He had discovered a passion for volleyball and student government and pursued them both. He became independent and rode his bike to and from school some days with his two amazing best friends. He walked his puppy and played with him every day and every night as the boy made good choices and grew into a responsible young man.

"Hey Mom!" he called out. "Mom! Can Gavin and I go fishing at the lake please?"

"I'm good with that. As long as you take the tunnel and don't try to run across the busy street with all your gear. What are you going to use for bait?" she called out while unpacking another box in the kitchen.

The puppy ran in, stole a big wad of crumpled newspaper, and dragged it out into the living room—an invitation to play.

"Hon, can you please come spend some playtime with 'puppy-chulo' before Gavin gets here? He needs some attention, and I don't want him to pee on the floor again while I'm unpacking."

"Yeah, sure Mom. I'll be right there."

The puppy ran in and began biting the corner of the box she was working on. He really was the cutest little guy, until his tiny razor-sharp teething bites locked into your soft flesh.

Her mind wandered as she unpacked the rest of the kitchen boxes with her new furry assistant. She thought long and hard about her son and was so proud of him, and of herself, really. She had escaped with her soul and sanity intact, aware that many who walked the long road of trauma suffered in silence, developing personality disorders from the vicious attacks. She had made it and was open to things being easier and more magical than she had ever imagined.

As fate would have it, her neighbors were heaven-sent. She absolutely thanked her lucky stars for the most beautiful woman next door. No stranger to trauma herself, Tina was recently widowed and appropriately pickled. The girl looked after the woman who would swerve while walking her little dog to and from the mailbox, drunk from her afternoon Mahjong tournaments or just from too many dry martinis and more chardonnay in her den while reading or watching her shows. They seemed to sense each other's pain still fresh beneath the surface, yet simultaneously respected one another's moxie and charm. It felt good to have a fresh start, and in this new chapter of her life, she understood that we either act out of fear or do things because we are clear. And life was good.

No longer in the struggle, she created new credos to serve her well in her new life. Rule number one: "Fuck what they think." Rule number two: "Bless and Release." With rules like these to guide her, she didn't need any more rules. In fact, what she needed was the opposite of rules. She needed to live a little. She suddenly felt in the mood for wild haute couture fashion and exotic drinks with new gay friends on sandy beaches in rich cities and spa-like resorts. She wanted room service at noon and then again at 2:00 a.m. in plush white fluffy robes after long hot lion claw baths. She wanted to hear the song of foreign tongues and see the smiles on different faces all around her. She wanted to live again.

Dilly invited her to an Ecstatic Dance party in Santa Monica with their friend Summer. She had heard a lot about these half-naked, vegan, crystal dance parties and wasn't sure how she felt, but she trusted Dilly. If nothing else, she would shop the bazaar tables in search of a long crystal necklace like the one Dilly got there that she admired so much.

The girl drove them up there in her new car, music fueling their enlivened conversation. It had been many moons since the girl had felt ecstatic about anything, let alone dancing—and sensually, at that! Summer vocalized how proud she was of the girl, and said she saw a palpable shift in her light and energy.

The girl took this compliment to heart, as Summer was tough as nails with a heart of gold but didn't blow sunshine up just any ass. She was a straight shooter, and also a single mother of a young son too. She knew what was up and had fought her own battles and lived to see the brighter side of life.

The girl swung them into the parking lot across from the address and they piled out of the car and headed to the spot. True to LA, there was a VIP list and the girl had to laugh. In another life, she had been a part of this world, with the Herbie Hancock's, Stevie Wonders, and Tina Turners of the Soka Gakkai Buddhist world, not far from where they were now. Or at Canter's, Damiano's, or Small's where she would lunch with Laura Dern, Erik Schrody, Christian Slater, Jake Dylan, Michael Richards, Diana Ross, Mickey Rourke, Carré Otis, Prince, or Madonna on any given day.

Dilly was in awe of all of the cute "spiritual" men who attended these gatherings. *This ought to be good*, thought the girl. The ceremony opened as they made a wide circle and began with a cacao mushroom elixir. Someone gonged as the whole room took one down and passed around, until the moment that all were in unison as they sipped the dark bitter elixir together, as one. This was magic. This was unity. This was electric life forever. This was needed.

The girl spent the next four hours swaying and arching, bending and looking around at all of the beautiful bodies in motion around her, sweating and writhing against the hardwood floors alongside complete strangers. The rules had been laid out clearly at the beginning of the ceremony: no drug or alcohol use, for obvious reasons. It was hard to keep to oneself with all this sexiness surrounding you, so the sober state made perfect sense. Beautiful, tight, fit, healthy Hollywood bodies covered with sweat glistened under rainbow lights. A trance-like spiritual DJ spun, as musicians played eclectic instruments around him, next to hired professional naked dancers on the two corners of the stage. The girl would occasionally stop and walk out of the great room, back into a small area with yoga lockers, a café, and rave-like blow-up furniture. There, mystics peddled their wares, as she looked for a crystal necklace that called to her. She bought one, only to give it to Dilly's daughter soon thereafter.

When the ecstatic dance was done, she realized as they walked out into the cold midnight air just how much it had been needed. It was an indication that she was free. She drove them all home safely and returned to unpacking and setting up the house with a renewed energy the next morning. For the first time in a very long time, life was good.

Her phone rang and she spoke to it without answering. She was too busy programming fare alerts on a hip travel app to care who called. Just the thought of being on an adventure brought her joy. She was ready to see the world again. There was a silly wiggle in her step and a song in her heart. In fact, she was totally geeking out! She was making up lyrics, singing to the puppy, and loving every moment of it. She felt like Judy Garland, Björk, and Velma all rolled into one. As if Phantom of the Opera was really a postmodern, one-woman show about how a single mother conquered the Me Too movement from her living room, set by McGee & Co for Elle Decor, music by Max Richter, the late Eazy-E, and Miss Honey Dijon, with choreography by the Black Dallas Dance Theatre. Oh yeah, it was going down in suburbia tonight. Tonight, and every other night after, she gave no fucks and lived-in neon. She was in a good mood and decided she liked being soft. She became a woman who would always smell faintly of vanilla, lavender, and cotton candy. She would do her best to nurture these soft feelings within her, for her highest well-being first, and then to share with her loved ones and help heal and inspire the world beyond.

This was how grace felt. This was her happy fucking ending. This was her manifesting new goodness to her in this moment and everyone to follow. She pretended to saddle the puppy and ride him around the room like a pony, singing, "My pretty pony, my pretty pony!"

"Mom! What the hell?" said the boy, surprising her as he bounded in through the front door.

"What's the matter? You don't like my pony showcase theatre? Poo-pay likes it, don't you poo-pay?" he sang.

"Mom! Stop it! G will be here any minute and I don't want him to see you dorking out! It's cringey!" he said, rolling his eyes.

"Lighten up sweetheart!" she sang, still smiling and dancing to an invisible beat, sliding and shuffling across the smooth marble floors.

"Weeeeeeeee!!! You should try this! It's fun!" she said, running and sliding across the floor in her socks.

It was truly a house party. The puppy picked up on her energy and began dooming zoomies around and around the living room. This made her son laugh and he joined in, chasing the puppy and making him run faster and faster around the coffee table.

"Watch out, you two! I don't want anyone getting hurt here!" she yelled as she connected her Bluetooth to a speaker and let music from The Gorillaz fill the air.

"I got sunshine in a bag / I'm useless, but not for long / The future is coming on . . . Finally, someone let me out of my cage! . . . Mystical, maybe . . ." Her archangel DJ was spinning the mix of her life. The beats spinning had her dork-dancing her heart out while day drinking, sipping Baileys on ice while music played on. "My future is coming on / It's coming on, it's coming on / My future is coming on!" She wore her medicine bag, now swinging around her neck wildly. It was like having an ecstatic dance party in her living room. Well, why not?

Her phone buzzed, and Dilly wanted to know if she wanted to come over this weekend and make tamales. Yes! They had never done it before, but right now? She was invincible! They would slay tamales! Spam callers buzzed her new iPhone 10 and she fake yelled at the device, "Alexa! Tell the spammers to go disappoint the next bitch! I'm busy!"

And so, it seemed that the girl had reached the proverbial light at the end of the tunnel. She had always fancied herself graciously "not most people" and could now add conqueror to the list. The queen of the underground was coming up, chasing the light, and feeling feather bright. It was a good day to ascend, a good day to be alive, and the perfect day to become the woman she had always known lived inside of her.

The girl took one last look around her and fully appreciated it. She knew that nothing a year from now would ever be the same. She would continue to grow and help others find their way. Darkness was a funny thing, when you thought about it; it seemed we had to have it in order to see the light that was always right there in the first place. Shadows had a valuable place in our lives, after all. No one outside the family had seen her crumble, but this brave new woman was determined that people would take notice as she began to rise. She felt good inside as she looked back at her triggers, thanked them for the lessons learned, and walked away stronger for it.

She was alone. But she was skinny, in a safe beautiful neighborhood, with an adorable puppy, some summer trips to look forward to, and the future wide open and bright ahead. Djedi never came. So, life wasn't perfect. In the end, she ended up losing far more than was ever gained. Now, she was tired and aged from the toll this had taken on her. Her body was stiffer and moved slower than it used to. Her spark was just a little dimmer. She wanted for nothing—well, just for time to go back to before the attack. She would rather have kept her job and have never been derailed in the first place. But such was life, and she would continue on her path with gratitude and do the best she could with her life experiences to help others and be of service. In the end, if she was strong enough to persevere and lift herself up out of this mess, then maybe, just maybe, she would be able to inspire or help just one other woman who was going through a similar situation. She wanted to tell all women: There are no rules and so you don't have to play by them. To teach them how to banish limiting beliefs as part of her core message. Maybe, she thought, she would just end up a vegan with a badass service dog, a best-selling novel under a pen name, and the peace from knowing she was able to provide and do right for herself and take care of her son and make damn sure he never ended up like them. Whatever her path, she felt she was close and that it was coming.

She could feel the blessings coursing through her whole body. How beautiful it was to be blessed by God. Blessed with breath, blessed with a heartbeat, blessed with the ability to feel everything so deeply. Blessed with sunlight, the moon and the stars. Blessed because the entire universe was supporting her every step. Yes, indeed, she was blessed.

She stood before the mirror above her altar on the side of her bed, and as she looked, she really saw herself. She saw all of it. The girl, the medicine woman, the love, the mother, the daughter, the friend, the artist, the writer, the editor, the colleague, the coach. She returned the gaze with confidence and said to her reflection, "The world needs your medicine, woman. You *are* amazing. You made it." She loved the person she had fought so hard to become.

She knelt before the altar and lit the large white candle with a white lighter from the drawer. Her crystals were arranged with purpose, designed to help manifest her heart's desire. As she called in her ancestors and gave them thanks, she also gave notice to each of the four corners—to the north, the south, the east, and the west. The scent of the candle and her oils filled her long deep breaths as a favorite poem of hers entitled "The Manifesto of Encouragement" by Danielle LaPorte came to mind. She reached down to one of her journals under the altar, opened to the poem and began to read:

"Right Now: There are Tibetan Buddhist monks in a temple in the Himalayas endlessly reciting mantras for the cessation of your suffering and for the flourishing of your happiness.

Someone you haven't met is already dreaming of adoring you.

Someone is writing a book that you will read in the next two years that will change how you look at life.

Nuns in the Alps are in endless vigil, praying for the Holy Spirit to alight the hearts of all of God's children.

Bless & Release

A farmer is looking at his organic crops and whispering, "nourish them."

Someone wants to kiss you, to hold you, to make tea for you. Someone is willing to lend you money, wants to know what your favorite food is, and treat you to a movie. Someone in your orbit has something immensely valuable to give you—for free.

Something is being invented this year that will change how your generation lives, communicates, heals and passes on.

The next great song is being rehearsed.

Thousands of people are doing yoga right now intentionally sending light out from their heart chakras and wrapping it around the earth. Millions of children are assuming everything is amazing and will always be that way.

Someone is in profound pain, and a few months from now, they'll be thriving like never before. They just can't see it from where they're at.

Someone who is craving to be partnered, to be acknowledged, to ARRIVE, will get precisely what they want—and even more. And because that gift will be so fantastical in its reach and sweetness, it will quite magically alter their memory of angsty longing and render it all "So worth the wait."

Someone has recently cracked open their joyous, genuine nature because they did the hard work of hauling years of oppression off their psyche—this luminosity is floating in the ether and is accessible to everyone.

Someone, just this second, wished for world peace, in earnest.

Someone is fighting the fight, so you don't have to.

Some civil servant is making sure you get your mail, and your garbage is picked up, that the trains are running on time, and that you are generally safe. Someone is dedicating their days to protecting your civil liberties and clean drinking water.

Someone is regaining their sanity. Someone is coming back from the dead. Someone is genuinely forgiving the seemingly unforgivable. Someone is curing the incurable.

You. Me. Some. One. Now."

This beautiful new woman who carried the light in her eyes, love in her smile, and wisdom in her bones was here to heal. She was a powerful force, a connector to ancient rites and cosmic channels. She folded her legs underneath her, releasing the pressure, raised her hands above her head, and clapped three times quickly. The candle went out, the book fell, the girl was gone . . . and only the woman remained.

The End

www.ingramcontent.com/pod-product-compliance
Lightning Source LLC
Chambersburg PA
CBHW050317120526
44592CB00014B/1947